WIRRAL GLEA

Including
Smuggling and "The Cave", Well Sinking,
Three Wirral Hills, Wirral's Olympic Marathon Runner,
Injustice in Birkenhead and A Wartime Fisherman.

by
GREG DAWSON

Author of the books 'Tingvelle', 'Arwe' and 'Wyrale'.

First Published 1998.

Copyright © Greg Dawson 1998

ISBN 0-9522598-3-4.

British Library Cataloguing-in-Publication Data.
A catalogue record for this book is available from the British Library.

Published by Dawson Publishing (of Irby).
Printed by INPRINT, King Street, Wallasey.
Typesetting by DAISYWHEEL, Bell Road, Wallasey.

£4.95

ACKNOWLEDGEMENTS

As always, I must thank all the "locals" for their enthusiastic help and interest. The oral history and anecdotes provided by local people are the backbone of my local history writings.

Thanks also to the Archivists and staff of Cheshire County Council Archives and Local Studies, Birkenhead Reference Library, Liverpool Museum and Liverpool Record Office, for the help and patience of their staff, and permission to use some of the documents from their collections.

My thanks also to the Public Records Office, Kew, Richmond, Surrey for allowing me to reproduce a page from the 1871 census of Upton, Wirral (3743).

Special thanks must go to two local historians, Geoffrey Place and Jim O'Neil for their help and invaluable advice.

My gratitude must also be expressed to those people who have been kind enough to pass to me documentary information, family letters and old newspaper cuttings etc.; Matt and June Wright, John Smyth, Paul Aird, Leo Carroll, Tim Budd, Malcolm Campbell, Alf Oxton, Dennis Kelly, my sister Geraldine Ryan and Fred Dashley of New Milton, Hampshire.

I am also very grateful to people who have been kind enough to loan me old photographs; Valerie Steel, Mark Evans, Henry Evans, Ian Boumphrey and Alan Smith and to David Patterson for sketching the well-sinking scene. Also a special thank you to my friend Peter Robinson of Heswall for his expertise and many hours of effort in taking photographs of various locations for this book.

Last but not least, I must thank my wife Jenny for supporting me in my hobby and thanks once again to her friend Dorothy Williams of Irby for her helpful comments and suggestions about my notes.

CONTENTS

COVER PHOTOGRAPH

The remains of Dawpool Quay. These sandstone blocks are situated on the shore between Thurstaston and Caldy. Hilbre Island can be seen on the horizon (1998).

ILLUSTRATIONS.

SMUGGLING AND "THE CAVE"

During the Middle Ages the River Dee at Chester became seriously silted up. This was due to a number of reasons including a weir built by the Normans which restricted the flow of the river, erosion of the coastline, shifting sands and a change in the world's climate which grew colder causing sea levels to drop. Eventually the water became so shallow that only small boats could reach the city.

The only way that Chester could stay alive as a port was for ships to anchor at smaller ports down river where the water was deeper. Passengers and cargo were then off-loaded and transported to Chester in small boats or by road.

At first the anchorage of Shotwick, only five miles from Chester was used but eventually this small port also silted up. Gradually ships were forced to move further along the Wirral coast to the deeper waters of Burton, Denhall and the "New Quay" at Lightfoots Pool, Neston. All ports along the Dee were referred to as the Port of Chester in shipping terms as they were under its jurisdiction.

Ships were being built progressively bigger making it hazardous for them to navigate the shallower waters of the lower Dee estuary. In the late 1600s Liverpool replaced Chester as Britain's second most important port. By 1700 the build up of silt around the New Quay made it difficult for large vessels to use Neston, the most important Deeside port. Chester's shipping was forced further away to deeper anchorages mainly at Parkgate, Gayton and Dawpool. From Parkgate and Dawpool, ferry boats called Packet ships sailed to Ireland. These Packet ships not only carried passengers but newspapers and cargo four times a week to Dublin. (The anchorage of Dawpool was close to where the Dee Sailing Club now stands on Thurstaston cliffs and was originally called Redbank).

The Chester shipping trade was worth a colossal amount and merchants were extremely worried about navigation. Vessels such as the Chester ship "Phenix" were known to have conveyed cargoes worth thousands of pounds to and from the Dee. In his will of 1702, Samuel Matthews of Neston leaves a half share in the ship "Phenix" and a third share in a boat, both of which were anchored at Caldy. His share in these vessels was together valued at £42. By comparison, this illustrates the value of cargo then estimated at thousands of pounds. The same goods would today be worth millions.

As time went on and the navigation became more difficult it became obvious that something would have to be done to prevent Chester dying as a port. A wide channel was dug from Chester along the Welsh Coast to deeper waters near Flint. This channel, known as the "New Cut", was 16 feet deep at high tide and when it opened in 1737 it became possible to navigate ships down to Chester City again.

The Irish Packet boats continued to operate from the anchorage at Parkgate. Because Parkgate was nearer the open sea, ferries could readily take advantage of favourable winds and sail straight out. It took two tides for large vessels to reach Chester City and another two tides to get out to sea again. Chester bound cargo vessels sailed in from the open sea as far as Parkgate or Flint before the tide turned and it became too shallow for them to continue. They then anchored and waited for the next tide and favourable wind to enable them to sail to the city via the New Cut.

Some of the larger merchant vessels had part of their cargo off-loaded onto smaller craft at Parkgate to make it easier for them to navigate the shallower waters at Chester City. If there was no favourable wind some ships were even towed down the New Cut. While these ships were at anchor at various places along the Dee Estuary, smugglers were given a golden opportunity to get contraband ashore.

Nearly all shipping operating from Chester and Wirral's Deeside ports went to and from Ireland, Wales, Isle of Man and London but a few vessels went to such places as Spain, Portugal, France, Holland, Russia and even Africa the West Indies and America. Welsh coal, cheese and leather from Chester, hops, oak timber, groceries, and large amounts of lead from the Halkyn Mountains in North Wales and trade goods were among the main exports of the day. Livestock, iron ore, timber, tobacco, coffee, tea, rum, brandy, wine, flax, linen, silk, lace, hides, soap etc., were among the main imports.

A further increase in Wirral's sea traffic came during the 1760s when a stone quay was built out into the river to enable coal sloops to tie up in a deep channel known as Colliery Gutter and load coal from Denhall Colliery at Ness. There was also a thriving shipyard at Parkgate which not only built various types of vessels but attracted others for repair, including Royal Navy yachts. Royal Navy ships and yachts escorted rich merchant ships to and from the Dee estuary as they were often at risk from foreign privateers and raiders which, during our wars with the Spanish and French, plagued the Irish Sea.

Vessels were even auctioned at Parkgate. The "Courant" newspaper 15th November 1768 advertised the Chester-built Snow "Nonpareil", about 120 tons and fitted out for the Irish trade, for auction at the "Golden Talbot Inn", Parkgate. All this varied sea traffic in and out gave local people a chance to acquire some smuggled luxuries. (A Snow is a type of Brig, with a foremast and mainmast carrying square sails, and a short mast immediately next to the mainmast carrying a fore-and-aft sail. A Talbot was an old breed of dog like a bloodhound).

Through much of the 1700s most smuggled goods came to Wirral and North Wales from the Isle of Man which had been ruled by the Stanley family, Earls of Derby and Lords of Mann since being given the Island by King Henry IV. Manx customs duties were extremely low, virtually duty-free, and contraband was run over in small fast boats and landed on the coasts of Wirral and North Wales. This went on until 1765 when the British Government bought the Lordship of Man for £70,000, and put a stop to wholesale smuggling. Most smuggled goods then came in from Ireland.

There were two types of smugglers, sea smugglers who brought the stuff in by sea and land smugglers, often well armed, who operated in gangs large and small transporting the goods inland. Land smugglers were ordinary tradesmen during the day and came together on certain nights when goods were landed on the coast. People living near the coast often deliberately acted innocently as if they were simple country folk. Down South one gang of men were found raking a river bed and when asked what they were doing they said that they were trying to get the cheese out of the river. The cheese they referred to was the reflection of the moon on the water. The customs men thought they were a bit simple and left them alone but in fact they were raking in kegs of brandy which had been hidden under water. This notorious gang later became known as the "Moonrakers".

Stonehouse wrote: *"Wirral up to the middle of the 18th century was a desperate region. The inhabitants were nearly all wreckers or smugglers. They ostensibly carried on the trade or calling of fishermen, farm labourers and small farmers"*. He went on... *"fine times the runners used to have in my younger days. Scarcely a house in North Wirral that could not provide a guest with a good stiff glass of brandy or Hollands"*.

The small band of customs men had the whole Dee coast as well as ships lying at anchor to search. High winds and heavy seas could drive sailing ships to anchor at any time, anywhere along the West Wirral coast from Hilbre to Shotwick and on dark nights or foggy days ships could be anywhere in the river. One of the customs men was a riding officer who patrolled the coast on horse-back.

Most of the accurate accounts of smuggling along the Dee coast come from records of smugglers and goods seized by the customs and excise men who took them to Chester or

Parkgate custom house. Other relevant information can be gleaned from old wills, land tax documents and old stories passed down through local seafaring families.

An extract from a letter written in the early 1700s by Sir Henry Bunbury, M.P. for Chester, to Sir Richard Middleton, M.P. for Denbigh, records the following reference to organised smuggling:

"Col. Manley says he has above two hogsheads of your wine that I have paid for so I hope you will think of leaving orders how it may be got by degrees when you are gone. We have had the divil to pay here on Monday morning. They seized 26 dozen at Park Gate, five of which are myne. Besides that the Lord knows how many pieces of Indian silk and Indian calico that the Irish ladies were running to make them fine at London this winter so now theyl be confined to their lodgings. I cannot get Mr. Vaughans wine yet out of the Custom House if it were to save my life". (A hogshead is a large cask containing 52½ gallons).

If this was how supposedly respectable Members of Parliament carried on it is not surprising that smuggling was rife.

One court case heard at the Quarter Sessions in 1757 concerns smuggled soap aboard a ship called the "Chester Paquet" which had arrived at Parkgate from Dublin. Customs men William Briscoe of Parkgate and William Saunders of Chester and others found forty six dozen parcels of soap concealed in the ship's ballast. The soap was taken ashore, loaded into a cart and taken to Parkgate Custom House. As the customs men were unloading the soap six or seven men came up, one had a whip and another a stick. They lashed the horses and drove the cart away with William Briscoe still in it. The customs men managed to stop the cart after a short chase and arrest the man with the stick. He was identified as John Lucas of Parkgate, a mariner aboard the "Chester Paquet". Lucas was prosecuted but the others involved escaped. More than likely the other men involved were shipmates of Lucas and considering the amount of soap involved, the Master, John McCullough of Parkgate, must have known about it. (In those days seamen were called mariners).

Most seizures of contraband were small but there were a few fairly large ones. The amount of goods smuggled is unknown as most were successfully disposed of. Contraband recovered by the customs men was auctioned off at the custom houses.

A number of sales of smuggled goods seized by customs men are recorded in old Chester newspapers. For example, "Adam's Weekly Courant" 3rd March 1767 records the following;
"To be sold, by order of the honourable commissioners of his Majesties Customs at the Custom House, Chester on Friday 6th of this said month March at four o'clock in the afternoon in several lots. One hundred and forty four gallons of brandy, thirty nine gallons of rum, twenty five pounds of tea and one pound of coffee.
And on Monday 9th at the Custom House, Parkgate at 12 noon thirty four gallons of brandy and five gallons of rum, in several lots publicly to the highest bidder. Samples may be seen at these places in the meantime".

Also in the "Courant" the following year during December 1768;
"To be sold at Chester Custom House, three gallons of brandy, three gallons of rum, two and a half pounds of coffee and twelve and a half gallons of Geneva.
At the Custom House, Parkgate on Friday 30th of this said month December at twelve of the clock noon, publicly to the highest bidder, Sixty three gallons of brandy, ten and a half gallons of Geneva, twenty and a half gallons of rum, two and a half gallons of whiskey, eighteen bundles and a half of printed paper, one hundred and ten yards of Irish printed linen, in remnants twenty yards of printed muslin, five hundred and thirty three yards of Irish poplin. The printed muslin and poplin are to be sold for exportation".
(Poplin is a corded fabric made of silk and wool. Geneva is a type of Dutch gin or schnapps distilled from grain and flavoured with juniper berries, it is also called Hollands).

They say that the customs and excise only recover a fraction of smuggled goods. Judging by the amount of contraband listed above, there must have been a fair amount of smuggling going on in Chester and along the West Wirral coast.

It appears that even some customs and excise officers may have been paying ships masters to bring goods in for them. In the will of Samuel Matthews, master of the Brig "Phenix" is a book of debts. Among the list of names owing him money are two customs and excise employees. Excise man Mr. Thompson owes Matthews nine shillings (45p) for cloth and brandy and Mr. Hughes the waiter owes him a £1.00. Both these sums were quite large in those days and it indicates that these men did "business" with Samuel Matthews. (A waiter was a customs officer properly called a "land waiter" who recorded goods landed ashore).

In the heyday of smuggling during the 1700s and early 1800s village populations were small. For example, in 1737 only seven births were recorded in Heswall-cum-Oldfield and Gayton. Three babies were born to mariners wives, and one each to the wives of a ships carpenter, blacksmith and yeoman farmer. The seventh child was born to a Heswall widow and is recorded as being *"the reputed daughter of David Burke of the Kingdom of Ireland"*. Even over 40 years later villages had hardly grown, land tax records of 1778 list 30 properties in Heswall and only 12 in Gayton. In such small close knit communities as Ness, Neston, Parkgate, Gayton and Heswall, all the beer-house and inn-keepers, boatmen, mariners, farmers and fishermen knew one another.

Many families were inter-related. This fact is illustrated in the will, dated 1779, of farmer Martha Totty, nee Simmons, widow of Heswall mariner John Totty. Martha leaves all her money, her house in Heswall called "Alice Prentons House" with an acre of land, two cows, some personal effects including silver etc., and a thirty second part or share in the Brig "Active" to her two granddaughters Mary and Elizabeth Wilkinson. She left her clock, walnut desk, pewter and several other personal effects to her son-in-law Thomas Wilkinson. If her two granddaughters were to die before the age of twenty, then Martha's estate was to be divided amongst other family. The names mentioned were her nephew Thomas Simmons, Mary Parr wife of John Parr, Ann Bartley wife of Thomas Bartley and the children of the late Mary Nield deceased and John Nield.

Thomas Simmons of Parkgate was master of the Brig "Active", John Nield was also a Parkgate ships master, John Parr was a Parkgate mariner, John Bartley was a West Kirby joiner and Thomas Wilkinson was a Heswall yeoman farmer.

The "Active" was a regular on the Parkgate to Dublin run returning with various cargoes including large amounts of linen. She was also known to have visited ports as far away as Marseilles in France. Martha Totty having a one thirty second share in the 130 ton "Active" was not unusual. Chester and Parkgate ships were often owned by a consortium of business friends and relatives who could nowhere near afford to own a vessel themselves. On the black side, if the vessel sank the loss was shared, on the bright side, especially with the Master being one of the family, these business partners were in a position to make their own money one way or another. (A Brig is a sailing vessel with two square-rigged masts and a fore-and-aft sail, or brigsail, aft of the mainmast).

All these local families helped one another and outsiders were not "in the know". The smuggling carried out in Heswall and Parkgate made a few local families a lot better off and gave many others a bit of a helping hand. Times were hard and most people were poor. Inn and beer-house keepers could not always make a living from selling drink and taking in lodgers alone, most were also small farmers, fishermen, wheelwrights, masons or boatmen etc. (Boatmen, in most cases, worked on small boats called lighters which were used to take passengers and cargo to and from larger vessels anchored offshore. Customs officers employed their own boatmen to take them out to search vessels in the river).

Most landings of contraband were small but by all accounts a nice little earner for a few but now and again there was a large operation, set up and run by unknown big-wigs. Much of the contraband destined for Parkgate, Neston and Chester was landed at night on the quiet beaches of Heswall and Gayton because Parkgate's waterfront was so open and busy with a road running along its length dotted with cottages, inns, lodging houses and, worst of all, a custom house.

Parkgate Waterfront.

On large operations smugglers rowed stuff ashore at night from their own boats, but smaller amounts of goods were hidden by crewmen aboard Irish Packet boats, Royal Navy vessels, coal sloops and cattle boats etc. Taking goods from a cattle boat or coal sloop was obviously easier than from a Packet boat as there were not usually any curious passengers to worry about. It was said that the crews of the Irish coal sloops made a few bob selling spirits to the rough and ready Neston miners.

When Irish Packet boats were at anchor in the river awaiting boatmen to come and take passengers, mail and cargo off, local fishermen came along-side, especially at night. The fishing boats would be fishing or just idly drifting by and waiting for the signal to pick up tobacco, spirits or cloth etc., from the larger vessels.

The Packet boat crew and fishermen were careful to carry out their business quietly so as not to draw attention to themselves. In the days of sail it could be difficult for a fisherman in a yawl to get close to a Packet boat. If it was a calm night, or a foggy day, a dinghy might be rowed out from the fishing boat to the larger vessel and goods lowered in.

When passengers were watching, one trick was for a crew member on the Packet to shout to a fisherman and ask to buy some baskets of fish. Some fish would be hauled aboard and brandy bottles or something would be lowered back down in the baskets after making sure the lids were flapped over. In many cases the goods were simply kept hidden onboard ship and rowed ashore at night when the coast was clear.

Many tales of smugglers and ghosts were passed down through local families including the Tottys. My cousin Frank Evans' wife Betty, nee Totty, is a Heswall farmer's daughter who knows a great deal about the area and remembers many tales passed down through her family. Kath Carruthers was also born and bred in Heswall. Her mother also was a member of the old Heswall farming family Totty, a name which goes back to the earliest records and could have come from the Viking name Tostig. Kath is elderly and has been in a home for quite a few years. She is in poor health now and her memory is bad these days. She knew a great deal about old Heswall and passed on many tales from older members of her family and luckily wrote a few down.

She was told that her mother's great-grandfather broke the family's farming tradition by running away to sea as a lad and eventually becoming Captain Henry Totty. He sailed from Parkgate and Holyhead to Ireland amongst other places and in the later 1700s sailed as master of several ships including the Irish Packets 'Murray', 'Hawke' and 'Leicester'.

Captain Henry Totty was indeed master of the above mentioned vessels but he was not the only seafarer in the family, in fact there were quite a few. If Henry Totty left a will, it is not in Cheshire County Council Record Office, but the wills of six of his seafaring relatives are, which just shows how much this local family was involved in our maritime history. Of the six Totty wills available, three belonged to mariners from Heswall and one each belong to relations from Parkgate, Neston and Caldy.

It was said that some pilots and ships' captains were involved in smuggling and that others were well paid to turn a blind eye to extra goods being loaded aboard in Ireland and later put over the side along the Wirral coast. The name Henry Totty appears on land tax documents of Heswall and Parkgate from the 1780s to 1801. When Captain Henry Totty retired he was reputed to have been a rich man and Kath wondered where he got his money from.

The whole of Parkgate was owned by Baronet Mostyn and Gayton was owned by the Glegg family who were Lords of the Manor. Other land owners owned most of Heswall and Neston, therefore not much local property came up for sale. Any mariner who made big money whether from smuggling, privateering, business or whatever, often had to keep hold of the cash, buy personal effects or invest in property elsewhere.

George Norman, a Parkgate pilot who died in 1801 aged 77 left his wife and granddaughters, four houses in Blundell Street, Liverpool. He also left £400 to his granddaughters Mary Anne and Betty Birchall and made a number of bequests to other family members leaving various amounts of between £20 and £50, silver shoe buckles and linen etc. His personal effects alone were valued at nearly £300, a small fortune in those days.

In 1801 Captain Henry Totty of Parkgate was the occupant of a "cottage and garden" owned by Baronet Mostyn which was assessed at one shilling and eight pence (8p) a year land tax. However, the properties leased by the seven customs and excise men were together assessed at 38 pounds and four shillings (£38.20p), a very considerable amount. For example, the will of one of the seven, Parkgate Custom House Officer John Humphreys, proves he was a rich man. He left all his *Real and Personal Estates and the Lands, hereditaments and premises situate and being in Great Neston* to his niece Margaret. Humphreys paid a personal land tax of £5, three of his fellow customs officers paid even more and the excise man paid twice as much. Also by comparison, at this period of time in the villages of Moreton, Upton and Irby, my own family owned five farms and leased three, paying a combined land tax of 15 pounds twelve shillings and six pence (£15.62½p), less than half the amount paid by the customs and excise men.

It was wondered how the customs and excise men could "earn" the money required to live in grand houses with lands. They were disliked by mariners and local villagers who thought that they were on a big wage plus "perks". Mariners worked hard often in stormy weather and when they eventually sailed into the Dee they resented the customs men searching their quarters and belongings for contraband. Many locals believed that not all contraband confiscated by customs and excise men went through the books.

It has always been said that pretty well all of the inter-related villagers in Parkgate, Gayton and Heswall Village (now the Lower Heswall) were "in the know" as regards smuggling. They reckon that even some of the clergy knew, and received wine. The customs men were seen as tyrants who were there to prevent poor locals getting a cheap drink or smoke. After a successful landing took place widows and old people might find a packet of tea, tobacco or something left on their step.

Heswall Lower Village.

Everybody watched for the movements of the customs men and kept a wall of silence. Even children carried messages with secret meanings. The password for an intended landing of smuggled goods on Heswall shore was "the ghost walks tonight". Legends and stories about ghosts were encouraged and this message had a double meaning. If anybody "not in the know" overheard anything then they would take the message literally and be scared away from desolate areas where contraband might be landed, transported or hidden.

There were a number of ghosts said to be seen in various places in the Heswall and Parkgate areas. In those days ghosts were called buggens, a name which appears to derive from the Welsh word "bwgan", a ghost. Smuggled goods taken from Parkgate to Neston were carried along Buggen Lane for obvious reasons. There was said to be the ghost of a headless dog on Barnston Common (now called Whitfield Common) and a big black dog on Heswall Beacons. The green ghost was said to roam Heswall Dales and the ghosts of two mariners who stabbed each other to death whilst smuggling goods were to be seen on Heswall shore. One version is that they fought to the death at the bottom of a path from Broad Lane in the "Bloody Gutter", a small fresh water stream which runs out onto the beach. Another version says the fight was in Manners Lane. It was also put about that the Devils black hearse could sometimes be seen along Cottage Lane and Well lane.

All these stories and more helped the smugglers as people kept away from these places at night. If anybody did mention seeing a man in a lane or on the shore, carrying or carting something they were usually told that it was such and such a ghost and that they were lucky to get home in one piece.

When a ship with contraband aboard sailed straight in from the open sea and dropped anchor for the night, it would be a while before customs men knew it was there. One of the best anchorages was in the deep waters of Gayton Hole, opposite the old cart track Manners Lane, which I believe was originally called Mariners Lane. Here, because of the slight inward curve of Heswall's coastline between Banks Road and Cottage Lane, a man standing back on the bank was not visible from the Custom House at Parkgate or the Watch House at Dawpool. When the coast was clear a lantern would be flashed from a field up on the river bank and the smugglers landed their contraband on Heswall shore.

Once landed ashore, smuggled goods were taken to secluded places and hidden overnight. The goods were rarely taken straight from the shore to an inn, farm or cottage in case the customs men were watching or following. Sometimes pack-horses were used to carry contraband, particularly spirits which often came in four gallon kegs. The next morning farmers drove sheep and cattle down the tracks and lanes to obliterate any trace of the smugglers "run".

The wild vast area of Heswall-cum-Oldfield Common, in those days covering over 500 acres of rugged land, including "The Dales" and "The Beacons", was usually where the smugglers headed for to hide their swag. Sometimes goods were dossed at other quiet well covered places such as "The Dungeons". As soon as the coast was clear the contraband was moved to customers, sometimes during the day hidden under cart loads of logs, turnips, hay or sheaves of corn etc. A farm worker could earn a weeks wages for transporting one load of contraband.

In those days there were only two dwellings anywhere near the shore, "Gayton Boat House Inn" and a small farmhouse called "Heswall Cottage" owned by the Church and occupied by the Barlow family. Only four lanes led to the shore, Broad Lane, Banks Road, Manners Lane and Cottage Lane which would have been the logical routes from the shore but these may have been watched by the customs men from time to time so the local men sometimes used another route. They followed the course of the little brook, years ago called the Scarbrook.

The smugglers would have followed the bushy course of the Scarbrook up from the Dee, through the rugged Dales to their most sheltered hide-out, a cave in a little dale near Thurstaston Road. The cave was made by the smugglers, cut out of a solid rock out-crop and big enough to hide goods and a small light dinghy. The entrance was hidden by bushes.

Usually the goods landed by Heswall men went to local customers but if there were any over they would be snapped up in Neston and surrounding villages. Goods from the larger landings organised by the big-wigs were believed to be taken to Chester by private coach.

In 1801 there were only 110 people living in Birkenhead and the combined population of Heswall-cum-Oldfield and Gayton was 268. Tranmere was Wirral's second largest village with 353 inhabitants but Great Neston (which included Parkgate) was by far the most populous town with 1,486 residents. Different goods went to different customers. Silks and linens etc., went to gentry and tailors. Wine, brandy, rum, whiskey, Geneva and tobacco went to local inns, beer-houses and gentry. The nearer the customer the better. The further the goods were transported the greater the risk.

Looking across the River Dee from Heswall Dales.

Looking from The Dungeon across Heswall Fields and the River Dee to Wales.

In the 1700s and early 1800s there were a number of beer-houses and inns in the area; in Parkgate were the "Golden Talbot", "Kings Arms" and a premises run by Richard Bartley which became known as the "Sawyers Arms", and others. In Gayton there were the "Old Three Pigeons" in Mill Lane and "Gayton Boat House Inn" situated at the bottom of Cottage Lane and run by the Crabb family. Situated in what is now Heswall Lower Village there were at least two beer-houses. They became known as the "White Lion" at the bottom of Wall Rake run by the Barlow family who were also farmers, blacksmiths and mariners, and the "Ship Inn" situated in Village Road. There was also a beer-house in Sandy Lane near what is now Heswall centre, in those days it was called Heswall-on-the-Hill or the Top Village and was made up of several small clusters of cottages. The "Anchor Inn" in Irby also had seafaring links. It was the nearest pub to Dawpool anchorage, about a mile and a half away and only a mile across the fields from "The Dungeon". These inns and beer-houses probably took delivery of smuggled spirits whenever possible in those days.

An old story in the Heswall area believed to be from somewhere between the mid 1700s and 1800, tells of armed customs and excise men having been tipped off about the smugglers cave and lying in wait for them to arrive with their contraband from a landing on Heswall shore. There were already some smugglers' wives waiting outside the cave with food and drink for their men. One version of the story is that customs men heard women's voices and thought the men were inside the cave sorting stuff out, so they crept up and shot the women and rushed the cave.

Kath Carruthers also passed this tale to my wife's Uncle Dennis. Her version was probably passed down through her family from her ancestor Captain Totty and is as follows:
"By the croquet lawn at the far side of the old house called "The Cave", Thurstaston Road, Heswall is a stone summer-house. Behind the walls of this summer-house is the large entrance to a cave, which was used by smugglers for overnight storage when a landing took place. One night some women were waiting by the cave for their men to bring the stuff from the shore. Excise men heard the women talking, crept up to them and shot them all dead, leaving their bodies there for the smugglers to find. It could only have been the excise men for nobody else had firearms. Excise men were armed with pistols and were like the Gestapo in their treatment of the people".

Although this story is quite strong I can find no written proof of a massacre. An incident as serious as that with a number of women shot dead would be documented somewhere. However, I would say something must have happened, but nothing so serious. Probably some kind of encounter between smugglers and or their women and customs men took place at the cave. The women might have heard or seen the customs officers creeping up on their men as they approached the cave and screamed to warn them and shots were fired, maybe by both sides, but the flintlock pistols used in those days were accurate only at close range. The customs men would have only got one or two shots off before everybody scattered across the Dales.

It would be difficult for a few customs and excise men to massacre a gang of women, even if they were ruthless enough to try. Maybe one woman was hit and when she eventually died, possibly years later of some other cause, people would always say that she never got over being shot by the customs men. As stories are told and re-told and time goes on, things are exaggerated with details getting more juicy. Certainly these were desperate and violent times. There are recorded cases in other areas of smugglers being shot dead by customs men and of customs men being murdered by gangs of smugglers.

Smuggling still carried on at Heswall but the cave was never used again for hiding stuff. As time passed children played there and farmers and woodsmen caught out by the weather sheltered in it. Graffiti gradually spread all over the walls from the 1800s to the present day.

The silting up of the River Dee's Wirral coast was greatly speeded up by the digging of the "New Cut" which altered the natural flow of the river. Parkgate's anchorage became too shallow for Irish Packet boats and the last one sailed in 1815. A proposal for shipping to transfer to Gayton Hole came to nothing and the Parkgate Irish Ferry service was transferred to Liverpool. Another proposal to run a steam ship service from a man-made sandstone harbour between Dawpool and Caldy was abandoned in 1822.

The Smugglers Cave.

There were still a few seamen living in Gayton. Heswall Church records list a child fathered by mariner Samuel Bennett in 1816 and several fathered by mariner Thomas Steens, one being in 1822. The tenants of "Gayton Boat House Inn", Margaret and William Crabb, were still there in 1818 as a child born to them is recorded in Heswall church records. The ferry service from Gayton to Flint was still running, but eventually it too stopped, and with the general run down in sea traffic, and being in an isolated spot, the inn closed and became a private house.

Over the years the numbers of customs men based at Parkgate varied but there were usually about half a dozen. Land tax records of 1801 record the following six custom house officers Barnes, Brown, Humphreys, Lewis, Monk and Williams and excise officer Jones. However with the reduction of sea traffic only one customs man was employed by 1820.

Chester and Welsh ports such as Saltney, Connah's Quay and Flint, along the deeper waters of the New Cut were still quite busy. But with only the odd cattle boat visiting Gayton and Parkgate or coal sloops sailing to Ness, smuggling became less and less. In 1853 Prime Minister Gladstone abolished customs duty on 123 items in his first budget, this together with the closure of Ness Colliery in 1855 was reckoned to have finished smuggling in Parkgate and Heswall.

As time passed, Liverpool merchants, cotton brokers and ship owners etc. came to live in the pleasant village of Heswall, famous for its clear fresh sea air. One such merchant was James Adam junior, a Liverpool fruit broker who bought land at "Dale Over". ("Dale Over" was a local name for the hillside on Thurstaston Road overlooking Heswall Dales).

James was the son of Scotsman James Adam senior, of Mount Vernon Green, West Derby, Liverpool. James senior was head of the successful Liverpool fruit brokers and merchants, James Adam, Son & Co. The company was founded in 1819 by his brothers Henry and William Adam. William lived in Lisbon, Portugal and shipped fruit to his brother Henry who ran the Liverpool end of the family business. William married the daughter of a Belgian who served in Portugal as Commissary-General to Lord Wellington, the Irish born commander of British forces fighting Napoleon. The Belgian became a naturalised Englishman, his name, De Bels, was given to William's son James, so that the name would live on through the male line. James in turn gave the Belgian name to his children and his family became known as De Bels Adam.

James Adam junior married his cousin Penelope Willet Adam, a sister of James De Bels Adam, in Lisbon on 2nd August 1859. James brought Penelope home to his native Liverpool where they started a family. The 1861 census of Liverpool records James Adam junior, a fruit broker aged 32, born in Liverpool, his wife Penelope aged 20 born in Portugal, their 6-month-old son Arthur De Bels Adam and three servants all living at 4 Grove Park, in the Rural District of Toxteth. Penelope had decided, like her brother, that she also wanted her Belgian grandfather's name to live on through her son.

The Adam family business was doing well and James junior and Penelope moved to a big country house called "The Ryffel" out in the well-to-do area of Woolton Park. By this time they had three daughters, Edith, Beatrice and baby Penelope, but unfortunately their only son little Arthur De Bels had died.

During the mid 1800s the small dale where the smugglers cave is situated was one of two small enclosures from Heswall Common together with two tree plantations close to Thurstaston road, rented from the Lords of the Manor of Heswall by Joseph Smallwood. Some of the Smallwoods had been mariners and were married into other local families including the Tottys. Joseph was a farmer who also worked as a wheelwright and ran a sandstone quarry. He grew hay in the dale and used timber from the tree plantations in his wheelwrights business which he ran from his timber yard in Village Road. Adjoining the tree plantations William Baxter Smallwood, tenant of the "Sandon Arms" in Heswall Slack also acquired a small enclosure.

James Adam's thriving business interests enabled him to buy the above enclosures and tree plantations totalling 1 acre, 3 roods and 19 perches to build a grand house. The land cost him £500 in October 1872 and work on the house started early in 1873 as an entry for February in the diary of Heswall farmer Henry Totty of "Lydiate Farm" records; *Mr. Adams building new house at "Dale Over"*. (One statute acre = 4,840 square yards, 1 acre = 4 roods, 1 rood = 40 perches).

The house was called "The Cave" after the smugglers' cave on the opposite side of the dale to the house. "The Cave" was to be a summer residence for the Adam family. It was designed by the architect John Francis Doyle and built on Thurstaston Road in a commanding position overlooking "The Dales" and the River Dee. To the north, on the corner of Oldfield road and Thurstaston Road, Doyle also built a house called the "Lodge" for Mr. Adam's coachman. Employed in the building of the new houses were a number of Heswall men including stone masons Thomas Edge, William Price, John and Joseph Smith, joiners George Lightfoot and George Totty and labourers Bill Collins and George Smith.

Up until the coach-house was built there was a large fresh-water pool in the woods to the north of "The Cave". The pool was fed by the tiny Scarbrook which drained some of the water from Poll Hill and what was then rough boggy ground between Thurstaston Road and Telegraph Road. The pool overflowed and the Scarbrook ran down through Heswall Dales to the River Dee. In 1873 some of the woods were cleared, the tiny lake was filled in and the brook diverted. Scarbrook became the fresh water supply to "The Cave", by diverting it into a large purpose built water tank which overflowed into a well in the grounds, which in turn overflowed and ran down the Dales.

When completed "The Cave" was, as it is today, a magnificent grand house with clear views of the Dee estuary and Welsh Hills. John Francis Doyle built the house out of local red sandstone and with a sturdy slate roof. He made seven rooms on the ground floor, six large bedrooms and two bathrooms on the second floor and another large bedroom (18' 3" x 15' 2") and a boxroom above. This tall solitary individually designed house with its seated stone porch and large thick oak door must have taken the ordinary locals' breath away as they stood and stared at what, a short time before, was a lonely spooky wood within the wild Dales.

During the 1870s James Adam bought five more small parcels of land, three adjoining "the Cave" and two on the opposite side of Thurstaston Road. The three adjoining plots were bought from James Lightfoot and Joseph Banks. The plot furthest to the south, purchased from Joseph Banks for £100 had a little old sandstone cottage on it. James Adam had this old dwelling extended for his gardener and called it "Cave Cottage".

The gardener's cottage was extended with character and the coachmans lodge was tastefully designed and well built. The stabling was built onto the "Lodge" and consisted of two stalls and a loose box with a loft above.

Architect Doyle was soon to be offered another mammoth building project in Heswall. On the evening of Sunday 19th September 1875 there was a violent thunderstorm in Heswall. Lightning struck the church during evening service killing two people, the organist and the bellows boy, and injuring several other worshippers. During the torrential downpour roads in the area were washed away, houses were flooded, livestock drowned and the road bridge over Barnston Dale was swept away. The church was severely damaged and to Doyle's design, eventually a new church was built onto the ancient tower. (The organist, 22 year old John Heveran of Athlone, Ireland, master at Neston National School, was buried at the church of St. Mary and St. Helen, Neston).

Farmer and Church Warden Henry Totty wrote in his diary on 27th June 1878: *"A stone laid in the New Church in which a bottle was inserted, in which bottle was deposited a London newspaper, a Liverpool newspaper, a shilling, a sixpence, a threepenny piece, a penny and a halfpenny. The name of the Rector, Henry Totty, Thomas Lea and the architect Doyle"*. The new church dedicated to St. Peter, patron saint of fishermen, was consecrated on 14th August 1879 by Bishop Kelly.

When the census of Heswall was recorded in April 1881, the Adam family were still living in Liverpool as it was too early in the year for them to come over to "The Cave" for the summer.

The only person recorded at "The Cave" was the gardener, William Jackson, a 66 year old widower from New Ross in Ireland, living in the gardener's cottage.

St. Peter's Church, Heswall. People tracing their ancestry might find the records of Heswall Church helpful as for some unknown reason during the 1700s, there were quite a number of marriages of couples from outside the area i.e. Liverpool, Tranmere, Bebington, Chester, Eastham and Wallasey etc., and also couples awaiting ship from Parkgate to Ireland.

Over in Liverpool James Adam and family had moved yet again to a big house called "Belem Tower" in Aigburth Drive, Sefton Park which was built on land leased from Liverpool Council for 75 years. In 1881 James was recorded as a 52 year old fruit broker and his wife Penelope was now 40. Their three daughters were there along with their cousin Fanny Adam from Croydon and four live-in maids and a cook. In "Belem Tower Coachhouse" was 52 year old coachman Edwin Bulfield from Cartmel, Lancashire and his wife Maria from Skelmersdale.

"Belem Tower" was named after the port area of Belem in Penelope's home city of Lisbon, Portugal where there is a castle called "Belem Tower" on the bank of the river Tagus.

Also listed in the 1881 census of Liverpool is James' business partner and cousin James De Bels Adam, a British subject born in Lisbon, Portugal. James De Bels Adam is recorded as being a 32-year-old fruit broker living at 80 Bentley Road, Princes Park with his 25 year old wife Jessie from Kent. They had three children, Camilla De Bels aged three, Harold De Bels aged two and Hilda De Bels aged one. Also at 80 Bentley Road were two live-in nurses Eliza Case from Liverpool and Elizabeth Taylor from Birkenhead, also a Welsh cook Jane Lloyd from Nantglyn and Irish waitress Fanny Buckley.

Fruit broker James Adam of "Belem Tower" and "The Cave" died on 13th May 1884 aged 55 and left his estate to his wife Penelope who carried on the tradition of living winter in Liverpool and summer in Heswall, bringing over their household staff, coach and horses. Her daughters looked forward to coming over to Wirral as they loved riding and ponies were brought over for that purpose. The girls rode the Dales and sometimes along the Dee coast as far as Chester and even into Wales.

In 1886 the railway network along the West Wirral coast was extended from Parkgate through Heswall to West Kirby where it joined the Hoylake to Birkenhead and Wallasey line. Heswall was now linked by rail to both Liverpool and Chester. This reliable regular transport was of great convenience to the Adam family and their visitors travelling to and from "The Cave". It also attracted many more Liverpool business people to Heswall and more houses, big and small, began to spring up in and around Heswall and Gayton.

In the busy spring and summer months a couple of extra local gardeners were taken on at "The Cave" as there was plenty of work for them. Woodland, fruit and vegetable gardens, greenhouses, flower gardens, a tennis court and a sloping croquet lawn laid in the little dale kept the gardeners busy. The new Heswall station also enabled the gardeners to send fresh produce from "The Cave" gardens in Heswall to "Belam Tower" in Liverpool.

The 1891 census shows us that Mrs. Penelope Willet Adam and family were still living at "Belem Tower" and that "The Cave" was being looked after by a new gardener and domestic servant, 58 year old Scotsman Robert Wilson and his wife Jane.

Meanwhile over in Liverpool the Adam family business was still thriving as they continued to efficiently supply fruit to their many big customers, including Robertsons the jam makers. One member of the family in particular was making a name for himself. Penelope's brother James De Bels Adam had become a senior partner having learned about the shipping side of things at Messrs. Lamport and Holt, Shipowners. He was the Past Master of several Freemason Lodges and served on the City Council, becoming Mayor of Liverpool in 1891 aged only 42. James De Bels was also Chief Magistrate and in 1892 became Justice of the Peace for the City. At this time he and his family lived at 6 Mossley Hill Drive, Sefton Park. Sadly, in 1897 aged only 47, James De Bels Adam died.

In Wirral during the 1890s another railway line was being laid, this time through the middle of the peninsula, linking Birkenhead to Chester. A new station opened in 1891 to service Heswall-on-the-Hill and was called Heswall Hills, although it was actually in the parish of Barnston. This extra station encouraged more Birkenhead, Wallasey and Liverpool people to move to the pleasant rural villages of Heswall, Gayton and Barnston. About this time the name of Thurstaston Road was for some reason or other changed to Gents Road, then back again in the early 1900s although it was always called Adams' Hill by the locals.

In 1871 two years before "The Cave" was built, Heswall's population was only 722. Owing to the railway network it rose to 2,167 by 1901. In 1904 Mrs. Adam paid the Lloyd family (owners of Heswall Dales) £1,765 for 21 acres 2 roods and 17 perches of the Dales adjoining "The Cave". Although other big houses had been built on the opposite side of Thurstaston Road "The Cave" was still in quite an isolated position. Fresh water was piped into the house at the turn of the century so that it was no-longer necessary to divert water from the Scarbrook.

The population of Heswall was 3,616 in 1911, a rise of 1,449 in 10 years, although this included patients of the Children's Hospital and boys of the Akbar Nautical School. As Heswall continued to grow rapidly the coming years were not kind to Mrs. Penelope Willet Adam. In 1915 she lost her youngest daughter Penelope, in 1916 she lost her nephew young Arthur De Bels Adam of "Brook Meadow", Childer Thornton (now a hotel and restaurant), on active service and in 1924 her eldest daughter Edith Charlotte died. But her friends and relatives visited her regularly. On summer nights during the 1920s and early '30s there were sometimes a number of big cars parked along the road outside "The Cave", at a time when there was hardly a car to be seen. The attraction which drew the well-to-do friends and relations of Penelope to visit in numbers on summer nights was the song of the nightingale. They sat out under the tall trees and listened to this rare bird for hours. In those days "The Cave" was sometimes fondly referred to by old Heswall folk as "the home of the nightingale".

Penelope and her daughter Beatrice must have enjoyed their summers in Heswall as year after year they followed the same old ritual, spending the winter months at "Belem Tower", Sefton and summer months at "The Cave", Heswall. In the days before the Mersey road tunnel was built they came over on the Mersey Luggage Ferry which was specially for the transportation of motor and horse drawn vehicles. The Captain of the Ferry took aboard the heavier vehicles first, such as loaded wagons and drays pulled by big shire horses which he arranged around the deck so to keep the boat on an even keel. When this was done he then signalled to the likes of the Adam family with servants in light wagonettes and cabs drawn by smaller horses and ponies. He waved them aboard and called down in a posh voice, "come along the swallows". In other words the summer visitors to Wirral, as just like swallows they returned home in Autumn.

When the Adam family returned to Liverpool, fresh fruit and vegetables from their gardens and fresh fish caught by Heswall fishermen were, as always, regularly sent over to them from the station in the Lower Village.

In 1934 Penelope Willet Adam died at "The Cave" aged 93. In her will she left some money to the minister of the Presbyterian Church in Myrtle Street, Liverpool but her entire estate was left to her surviving daughter Beatrice Maud Adam and her nephew Harold De Bels Adam was an executor.

After her mother died Beatrice found that "Belem Tower" was too big for her so it was sold and she moved to "Meleb", ("Belem" spelt backwards) 26 Croxteth Road, Liverpool. "Belem Tower" was eventually demolished and Liverpool Corporation built a block of flats on the site called Belem Tower giving the City its first "tower block".

Beatrice carried on the seasonal migrations between Liverpool and Heswall, with her maid Lily Ireland, who was also her companion. Although it was now a modern era there was still no electricity in "The Cave" except in the kitchen as the maid refused to go there unless some modern services were installed.

Periodically, from 1935 onward, Beatrice sold off several parcels of land. One of these was a one acre plot on which "Gilstead", Oldfield Road was built. In later years a further plot was sold to enlarge the grounds of this house. Permission was also given to divert the Scarbrook into the grounds of "Gilstead" to make a water garden.

By this time the smugglers' sandstone cave was well and truly etched with dates and initials of children from the Adam family and local lads who wandered up the dale and played in it. Ciggy Wakelam, a local man, recalls as a lad before the war, seeing a statue of the Virgin Mary in the cave when he sneaked in there for a sly smoke or to play truant from school during the 1930s.

In July 1959 Beatrice Maud Adam, the last of her branch of the Adam family, died aged 92. She left the bulk of her estate to be divided equally between several of her cousins. You can tell by her will that she was a kind, caring person as she made quite a number of bequests, leaving treasured jewellery and china etc., and sums of money, large and small, to servants, friends and relatives from all over the country and as far away as Canada. She also bequeathed money to the Presbyterian Churches of London, Maghull and Heswall and to a number of charities including Dr. Barnardo's Home, British Limbless Ex-servicemen, Liverpool Spastic Fellowship, the Society for the Blind, and the Institute of Research for the Prevention of Disease in the City of Liverpool.

"The Cave", her father's individually designed grand house, its lodge, gardener's cottage, most of the original grounds and land which included a fair portion of Heswall Dales, totalling about 21 acres was put up for auction in September of that year and sold for only £12,700.

When "The Cave" came up for sale the Dales Syndicate had the foresight to buy the house and land to stop builders demolishing it and building on its dales and grounds. The Dales Syndicate was formed by Mr. Critten. This noble body, made up of 20 people whose houses overlooked "The Cave" and its grounds chipped in what they could each afford. They were, R.J. Critten, Sir Ernest Stacey, Mrs. M. Mellor, Miss M. Alexander, E. Billington, J.Rawlinson, A.B. Paterson, E.T. Elton, J.C. MacGregor, E.R. Furbur, G. Thomas, W. Storey, O.C. Dixon, A.J. Wannop, G.I. Robb, C.D. Whitnell, E.R. Crawford, T.H. Smeddles, E.N. Ridgeway and Mrs. Ravenscroft.

They bought Adam's former estate for £12,700 and also paid various legal fees, maintenance and other bills amounting to £1,100. "The Cave" with two acres of land was sold separately, as was the Lodge and adjoining stables called "Palfreyman". Mr. Critten acquired the former gardener's home, "Cave Cottage". A number of members of the syndicate bought parcels of land so to box "The Dales" in from developers. The remaining land, amounting to about 15 acres of Dales, was given to the Council for the use and enjoyment of the people of Heswall. During the mid 1970s Wirral Urban District Council bought "Dale Farm" and the rest of the Dales from the Lloyd Trustees. This large area of rough heathland covered by heather, gorse, trees and rocks with paths criss-crossing and intersected by several dales, makes up a unique area of natural beauty.

In 1982 "The Cave" and its two acres of land which included the little dale where the smugglers' cave is situated, came up for sale again. Liverpool business people Matt and June Wright bought the old Victorian house in October of that year and set about renovating it. Eventually they moved in on 24th May 1983. Since then Matt and June have spent countless hours and money restoring this unique merchant's summer residence to its former glory. Everything is as it was, immaculate and tastefully furnished making each room a delight to enter and view.

Matt and June have bought a further piece of land and they now own four acres of the original grounds. The old croquet lawn is still there in the floor of the dale, flat but sloping down hill with the lie of the land, but the old stone summer-house built for the Adams has long since vanished. The bridge which James Adam had built across the Scarbrook was dismantled many years ago when the little stream was diverted. However, the gardens are largely restored to the original layout and many big trees of the two original plantations recorded on the tithe map of 1849 still survive.

The old cave in the rock face under tall trees would have been well hidden by bushes and ferns a couple of centuries ago when this spot was part of the wild Dales. Cut out of a solid sandstone outcrop in the side of the little dale, the cave is fascinating to enter. The doorway is five feet nine inches high and two foot six inches wide opening out into an oval shaped room measuring 8 feet 6 inches wide, 9 feet 7 inches long and 6 feet 1 inch high. The sandstone walls have been cut to form a rock seat or bench 18 inches high and 16 inches wide around most of the perimeter of the room with the shapes of a stem and stern chiselled out at opposite sides of the cave to accommodate a dinghy of nearly 8 feet long. The raised rock level in the form of a perimeter bench must have been not only to sit on but to stack perishable goods as the cave has been known to flood during a torrential downpour.

"The Cave", built for Liverpool merchant and fruitbroker, James Adam.

The exact age of the cave can only be guessed at. Inside the cave Matt and myself were baffled by the many rope-like veins of rock running down the smooth walls. We invited archeologist Rob Philpott of Liverpool Museum to come and see the cave and perhaps calculate its age. Rob said that the veins of rock appear to have been made by rainwater washing quartz like minerals down cracks, forming hard deposits along their length. Over the years rainwater seeping through and running down the walls of the cave has probably eroded the sandstone leaving the hard deposits to stand out like veins. I asked Rob how long he thought it would take for veins as prominent as these to form but it was impossible for him to make an accurate calculation. It has been said that the cave is well over 200 years old, so it could have been cut out around 1750 or even earlier. Authentic dates chiselled into the rock start in the 1800s, some markings are very faint and older ones might have been washed away. But as Rob pointed out, no smuggler in his right mind would cut his initials and the date in a hide-out.

Today Heswall is no longer a village but a town with a large population made up mostly of families from outside the area. In the early 1800s a number of large local families including Ainsworth, Barlow, Boumphrey, Birch, Briscoe, Crabb, Edge, Ellis, Hough, Lawton, Lightfoot, Price, Rutter, Swift, Tarbuck, Taylor, Smallwood and Totty made up about half the population of Heswall and Gayton. As local farmers used to say in my grandfathers day, "throw a stone in Heswall Bottom Village and you'll hit a Totty, throw one in Neston and you'll hit a Jellicoe". So much has changed in the Heswall area since those days, which is to be expected, but there is still a lot to see and there are walks through yesteryear to enjoy.

The dark patch under the bushes in the centre is the entrance to the Smugglers Cave.

The doorway of the Smugglers Cave showing the inside lit up.

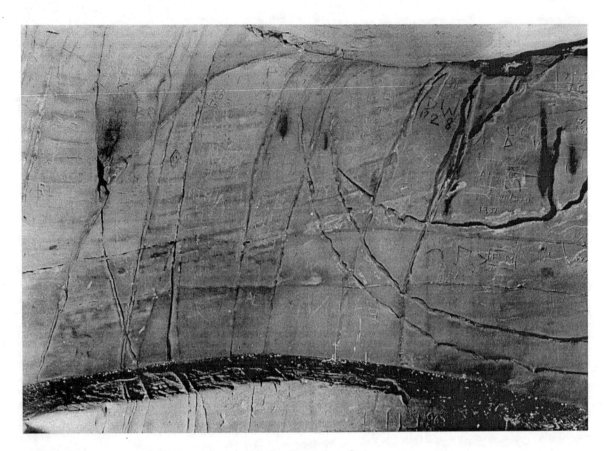

Inside the Smugglers Cave.

The odd ghost is still seen every now and again. One night Ciggy Wakelam and his wife were driving home from the "Dee View" via Thurstaston Road. When they reached Queens Drive a strange woman dressed in either black or dark green, wearing a long skirt, shawl and bonnet, crossed the road in front of them and disappeared through a solid sandstone wall. Could she have been the ghost of a smuggler's wife shot outside the cave or the green ghost?

To appreciate and enjoy what's left of Wirral's character and beauty you have to walk. A copy of the "A to Z" for under £3.00 and in full colour is a pocket-sized priceless investment when driving or cycling to various places off the beaten track where you want to walk around. They show the footpaths and landmarks and name all roads which enables you to park in the right places. With an "A to Z" you can't get lost.

A wander from Telegraph Road down Thurstaston Road through Heswall Dales passes an hour and is an interesting enough walk with very pleasant views. The large green at the junction of the two roads mentioned above was once a boggy triangular piece of the huge Heswall-cum-Oldfield Common, which still covered 476 acres as late as 1849. At the far end of this green, the source of the ancient Scarbrook can be seen running from under Telegraph Road and forming the boundary between the green and the garden of "Speedwell", Thurstaston Road.

Further down Thurstaston Road at its junction with Oldfield Road is the individually designed "Palfreyman". This former Lodge and stables of "The Cave" was where Mr. Adam's coachman lived. It is full of character and even the name brings back yesteryear. (A palfrey is an old name for a riding pony).

Further along Thurstaston Road is the magnificent "Cave" itself, better seen than described. The building of "The Cave" and St. Peters Church have given the people of Heswall lasting monuments to the all round architectural talents of John Francis Doyle of 4 Harrington Street, Liverpool. Doyle was born in Liverpool, a descendant of an Irish family which had settled in

- 20 -

the City in the early 1800s. Over the years he built, enlarged, altered and tastefully restored many churches, schools, private residences and commercial buildings. Some of the churches were Neston, Heswall, Tranmere, Wallasey, Maghull, Halton View; St. Ambrose, Widnes and St. Luke's the Evangelist, Walton etc. Also rectories at Barnston, Waverton and Helsby etc., and Dawpool School, Thurstaston. The private residences include The Roscote and The Cave, Heswall; Gildruce, Noctorum; Gleddill, Sefton Park; Residence at Alexandria, Egypt; The Willows near Windsor for the Dowager Duchess of Sutherland, Tan-y-Bryn at Bangor for Lord Penrhyn and the Grand Hotel, Llandudno. He also built a number of commercial buildings including Accrington New Market Hall, the North and South Wales Bank Buildings in Rhyl and Liverpool; the Bank of Liverpool, East Branch; Martins Bank, Edge Hill; the White Star Buildings, James Street and The Strand; The Commercial Fruit Sale Rooms in Victoria Street, Liverpool; the Royal Insurance building and the Cotton Exchange etc.

Matt and June outside "The Cave" with their 1921 Silver Ghost which took seven years to restore after lying in a scrap yard for 12 years. Matt has many hobbies including a life-long interest in restoring old cars like the Silver Ghost. He has also had many years experience in the military having been in the Royal Artillery Territorial Army and the Royal Naval Reserve.

Just past Matt and June's grand house is "Cave Cottage" the former gardener's tied cottage, in a nice secluded spot and now extended.

A short distance down the road, less than 20 paces before Queens Drive, between the sandstone wall of "Lingmel" and a hedge, is a narrow sign-posted path leading into "The Dales", now a nature reserve. Follow the footpath down to the "Smugglers Dale". After a short distance you come to the Scarbrook which only flows well in wet weather, most of the time it only trickles down from the private grounds of "The Cave" and sometimes it is dry. Don't cross the tiny bridge made of two railway sleepers, take the path to the left just before the brook which soon flows under a fence into a nice private water garden. Follow the path through the trees and down the dale. You can see why this hidden route would have been favoured by smugglers bringing goods up from the shore in years gone by. In those days there was hardly a cottage anywhere near and both sides of the dale would have been wooded with silver birch, rowan, oak and thorn bushes.

The smugglers' path comes out into open ground and ahead you can see Bush Way off Pipers Lane. A broad path with wooden railings leads into "The Dales" from Bush Way. On reaching this path go through the railings and walk to the right up the hill into the heart of "The Dales". There are grand views of the River Dee and Wales from the higher ground. The path eventually comes out onto Oldfield Road which leads back to Thurstaston Road and the green on Telegraph Road.

"The Dales" are a nice place to wander for a while, full of colour with red sandstone rocks, cliffs, gorse, heather and various trees and bushes here and there. There's also a bit of wildlife including the odd lizard, I've even seen a pair of ravens there. When over 500 acres around this area were wild heathland it's easy to see why smugglers chose to hide their goods here.

Another walk with pleasant views, in the former haunts of smugglers can start in the public car park in Banks Road close to what is now "Sheldrakes" restaurant, formerly Heswall Sailing Club. From Banks Road to Parkgate "Boathouse" and back is four miles, if you carry on and walk the length of Parkgate Parade and back it is nearer five and a half.

The walk starts from the shore at "Sheldrakes" and leads to Parkgate. In wet weather be sure to wear wellies or boots. From here it can be noted how the riverbank curves inland concealing it from the view of both Parkgate and Thurstaston, which is why it was a landing place for smugglers. Unfortunately the only boats you will see now are pleasure craft and fishing nobbies moored in what's left of Gayton Gutter, once the main channel to Parkgate and Chester. This coastline was very lonely in years gone by. In 1849, along the riverbank from Thurstaston to the edge of Parkgate and for nearly half a mile inland, there were still only two houses. "Heswall Cottage" which stood between Banks Road and Manners Lane became derelict and was demolished, so that as late as 1870, along four miles of coastline there was only one house, "Gayton Cottage".

After passing the small promenade at the bottom of Parkwest and eventually another one at Riverbank Road, keep walking beside the old sea wall until you reach the bottom of Cottage Lane at Walls End. Here stands "Gayton Cottage" which was once the "Gayton Boat House Inn" from where a ferry sailed to Flint for over 600 years. The Crabbs, a very old Gayton seafaring and farming family, were publicans of this old inn. When it closed William Crabb eventually took the tenancy of the "Glegg Arms" when it was built in the 1830s. In later years George Crabb took over. He must have been about a bit, as three of his children were born in Peru.

Meanwhile "Gayton Cottage" was made into a private house and became the home of John Baskervyle Glegg Esquire junior. In the later 1800s "Gayton Cottage" became the home of retired shipbuilder James Fergusson of Dunfries and during the early decades of this century Leonard Brooke the cotton broker and punt-gunner lived here.

Sandstone steps lead up from Cottage Lane onto the sea wall. The mile walk from here along the old sandstone sea wall to Parkgate is particularly pleasant, breezy and dry. With Heswall golf course on one side of the path and Gayton Marsh on the other, the views are uninterrupted.

After about half a mile you come to an old slipway beside a small brook where I believe Irish, Manx and Welsh livestock came ashore. The cattle boats anchored offshore in Gayton Gutter and cattle, horses and ponies were put over the side to swim ashore and scramble up the slipway. They say that pigs and sheep had their legs tied and were rowed ashore. The brook beside the slipway marks the ancient boundary between Gayton and Leighton.

Gayton Gutter at Heswall Shore. In the days before the spread of the marsh the tide came right up to the river bank. This inward curve of the coast between Banks Road and Cottage Lane was where the smugglers usually landed their contraband.

Riverbank Road car park, less than 1½ miles from Parkgate is a handy place to park when going for walks along the West Wirral coast. This view looking down the slipway towards Shelldrakes Restaurant, Banks Road pictures an area, which, in living memory has been transformed from golden sands to marshland. What is left of the ancient anchorage of Gayton Hole in Gayton Gutter is now a narrow tidal creek to the left of the picture.

Gayton Cottage, once Gayton Boat House Inn standing at the bottom of Cottage Lane.
For over 600 years a ferry sailed from here to Flint.

Walls End, Cottage Lane. These ancient sandstone steps leading up onto the old sea wall were well trod by seafarers and travellers in years gone by. Today they are the start of a pleasant dry one mile walk to Parkgate.

A short distance from the old slipway the sea wall path leads into part of the Wirral Country Park and carpark which is built on what was once Parkgate swimming baths. The nearby "Boathouse Restaurant" is built on the site of the "Pengwern Arms" which was pulled down due to storm damage. From here a ferry service sailed to Flint and Bagillt until 1864. The walk of just over half a mile along the length of The Parade is recommended as there are so many old buildings to see including fishermen's cottages, pubs, the "Watch House" and shops where fresh shrimps and home-made ice cream can be bought. It's strange to see an old seaport with no sea. But still, it's easy to imagine how it must have been years ago especially if you happen to be there on one of those rare occasions when a high spring tide comes up to the sea wall.

Gayton Slipway situated in the sea wall at the end of Heswall golf course, is where Irish, Manx and Welsh livestock scrambled ashore.

Also from Banks Road and "Shelldrakes" travelling in the opposite direction is another good walk of three and a half miles along the cliffs to "Sally's Cottage" at Thurstaston and back along the sandy beach. Or, if you are feeling energetic and have the time to spare, you can carry on and walk to Caldy and back, which is about six miles.

Start by walking along the shore and past Heswall Boatyard towards Thurstaston. Amongst the craft at anchor in Gayton Gutter you will often see the fishing nobby "Blue Circle" belonging to an old mate of mine, Henry Evans, a descendant of one of the oldest Dee fishing families. After walking about half a mile you come to the Dungeon Brook which runs out onto the beach. Years ago this part of the brook was called the "Bloody Gutter" as it was said to be where two smugglers fell out and fought to the death. They say that smugglers carried their contraband along the course of this brook to "The Dungeon" or along Broad Lane, via what is now Target Road and up to "The Dales".

This isolated spot, years ago called Heswall Point, was an old anchorage and has ties with history ancient and modern. A footpath runs from here to the bottom end of Broad Lane which, from Target Road onward, was once called Warmby Lane. This can be seen on the 1831 map of Wirral. This area is said to be the possible site of a Viking settlement. The name Warmby,

Two regulars in Gayton Gutter close to Sheldrakes Restaurant, Banks Road, the "Scotch Mist" and Henry Evans' shrimping nobby the "Blue Circle".

Heswall Boatyard after the severe storm of 1990. Under extreme weather conditions the sea can still lash Heswall Shore. The Nobby on its side is the "Josephine" which belonged to the late Laddie Evans and had been washed out of the Boatyard.

meaning "warm farmstead", ties in with other Viking names in the area i.e., Irby, Pensby, Frankby and West Kirby etc. The bottom of Broad Lane being in a sheltered spot with good flat farmland and fresh water available from the "Bloody Gutter", all add weight to the possibility of there once being a Viking settlement here.

Today, the "Bloody Gutter" runs into the riveted steel hull of an old wrecked lifeboat which belonged to fisherman Roy Mealor of Parkgate. Roy used to moor the lifeboat out in the estuary where, over several days, he filled it with cockles, then towed it to shore with his nobby. During a winter gale in about 1960 it broke from its moorings and was holed by boulders and sank where it is today. Further along the shore is the old wreck of the nobby "Shrimp Girl" which belonged to Bill Norman of Willaston.

At the "Bloody Gutter" a wide gravel bridle path leads up steps onto the river bank into the "Far Ends" now called "Heswall Fields", where one branch goes to the Wirral Way and the other along the cliffs. From here "The Dungeon" is visible on the hillside. This little wooded dale, with its rocky brook and waterfall, was said to be a haunt of smugglers and also where fishermen and mariners hid from the press gangs. The walk along the cliffs is easy and pleasant with some of the finest views in Wirral.

After covering about one and three quarter miles from Banks Road you come to the Wirral Country Park, with its Visitors Centre and cafe, which are both worth a visit. At the very bottom of Station Road a path goes through bushes and down steps to Sally McCrae's old cottage on Thurstaston shore. I believe this isolated cottage was once a Watch House which must have had a stable as the customs man stationed here was a riding officer. In the early years of this century an old wildfowler named Smith lodged here, he was better known as "The Lord Be With You" as that was all he said to anyone he met on the marsh whilst out shooting with his 4-bore.

Thurstaston Shore and Shore Cottage (centre). A path from the bottom of Station Road leads down steps onto this beach below the Wirral Country Park.

Shore Cottage, better known as Sally's Cottage. Customs men stationed at (Dalpool) Dawpool anchorage lived in this former Watch House. According to the 1769 Liverpool Directory, riding officer William Parkinson was stationed at Dawpool.

Half a mile further on just past the road leading up the cliffs to the Dee Sailing Club you will notice a lot of big sandstone blocks along the beach. These blocks are what is left of a quay wall built at Dawpool. Years ago a lad I know found 30-odd old well worn silver coins and as many copper ones near this spot. A short distance further on are Caldy Steps where you can sit and relax and enjoy good views of Wales, Hilbre Island and the Dee estuary before returning to Banks Road.

The walks along the Dee are very pleasant and my wife Jenny and I enjoy them (often returning via the Wirral Way). But it's sad that the marsh, creeping further and further along the coast, has robbed us of our sandy beaches, fishing and seafaring communities.

Over the centuries a large number of young mariners from our local villages left these shores to try and make something of themselves, one way or another and unfortunately many never returned.

Information gleaned from old wills and church records sometimes tells us fascinating facts about some seafarers. In some cases the ships they served and died aboard are named, how far they sailed and who their family were. Examples being; William Rutter of Heswall who died aboard H.M.S. "New York" in 1712 and left all his belongings to his mother Ann. My ancestor Simon Dawson of Irby who died in 1725 aboard an un-named ship and left all his possessions to Nathaniel his *"natural and lawful brother"*. Richard Ainsworth of Heswall who died in 1737 off the coast of Virginia and left his belongings to his sister Grace. William Totty of Parkgate serving aboard His Majesty's Yacht "Dublin" left his wages and belongings to his wife Mary Totty alias Ainsworth and his children, William, Martha and Henry in 1746. Thomas Webster of Neston had served aboard His Majesty's Ships "Superb" and "Deptford" when *"owing to the perils of the sea"* he made a will before dying aboard the "Antelope" in 1748 and left all his wages, tickets and bounty money etc., to his wife Elizabeth of Ness.

George Taylor of Neston who died aboard *"the good ship the "Snapper" trading to the coast of Guinea"*. David Gibbons from Brunswick in New England died in 1764 aboard the Brig "Hawk" anchored at Dawpool. Ann Bedson of Neston, one of the few female mariners in those days, died in 1765 aboard an un-named ship and left all her belongings to William Leach and Edward Robinson.

Sandstone blocks on the shore between Thurstaston and Caldy are all that is left of Dawpool Quay.

Unfortunately the days of the regular arrival of Packet boats etc., smuggling and cheap strong drinks sold in local inns to villagers who didn't care tuppence where it came from, have long gone. Sadly, all the pubs I have mentioned in the smuggling era have long since closed, except for the "Anchor Inn" at Irby.

In the 1960s I often had a few pints with local men in their 70s and 80s who told me quite a few tales passed down to them from their grandparents and great-grandparents, many of whom sailed in and out of the Dee. Obviously, with the passage of time and stories being retold by different generations, some accuracy is lost. But there is always some truth even in the most surprising tales.

There are old stories of fugitives wanted by the law in England being hidden aboard coal sloops at Ness and smuggled over to Ireland. Also of men wanted in Ireland being put ashore along the Dee from sloops and cattle boats. Friends, relations or money could get people away, then, as now.

The last cargoes I know of being landed on the Dee coast of Wirral other than fish catches, were at Parkgate, Heswall and West Kirby. Dr. Lewis McAfee of Grange Hill, West Kirby tells me that as a boy in the early 1890s his father saw a cargo of coal, probably from the Point of Ayr Colliery, landed ashore from a lighter at West Kirby Sailing Club. Also, into the 1890s small flats came over from Ireland with cargoes of turnips which were landed at high tide on Parkgate middle slip. The flats then steamed straight back to Ireland. Welsh boats also came in and dropped rock off for road building. At the turn of the century bricks and tiles from Buckley Brickworks were landed at Heswall to build the cottages along Banks Road. Then it became too shallow even for these small craft. (Flats are small flat-bottomed vessels used for navigating shallow waters).

Sawyers Cottage facing, as seen from Parkgate Parade. This neat old cottage was formerly a beer-house called the Sawyers Arms, a popular haunt of smugglers.

Today even the "New Cut" is silted up but the odd coaster can still get along the Welsh coast as far as Shotton Steelworks when there is a very high tide. Sadly our Wirral ports have been dead to all but fishing for a century. There's not much left to remind us of the days when the Dee was busy with Packet boats, Cargo ships, Royal Naval vessels and fishing boats, just a few old buildings, sea walls, plenty of old tales and the "Smugglers' Cave".

A SMUGGLERS SONG

If you wake at midnight and hear a horse's feet,
Don't go drawing back the blind, or looking in the street,
Them that asks no questions isn't told a lie.
Watch the wall, my darling, while the Gentlemen go by!
  Five and twenty ponies,
  Trotting through the dark -
  Brandy for the Parson,
  'Baccy for the Clerk;
  Laces for a Lady; Letters for a spy,
And watch the wall, my darling, while the Gentlemen go by!

Running round the woodlump if you chance to find,
Little barrels, roped and tarred, all full of brandy-wine;
Don't you shout to come and look, nor take 'em for your play;
Put the brushwood back again, - and they'll be gone next day!

If you see a stableyard setting open wide;
If you see a tired horse lying down inside;
If your mother mends a coat cut about and tore;
If the lining's wet and warm - don't you ask no more!

If you meet King George's men, dressed in blue and red,
You be careful what you say, and mindful what is said.
If they call you "pretty maid", and chuck you 'neath the chin,
Don't you tell where no one is, nor yet where no one's been!

Knocks and footsteps round the house - whistles after dark -
You've no call for running out till the housedogs bark.
Trusty's here and Pinchers's here, and see how dumb they lie -
They don't fret to follow when the Gentlemen go by!

If you do as you've been told, likely there's a chance,
You'll be give a dainty doll, all the way from France,
With cap of Valenciennes, and velvet hood -
A present from the Gentlemen, along o' being good!
  Five and twenty ponies,
  Trotting through the dark -
  Brandy for the Parson,
  'Baccy for the Clerk.
Them that asks no questions isn't told a lie,
Watch the wall, my darling, while the Gentlemen go by!

Rudyard Kipling.

WELL SINKING

The most important thing for any settlement anywhere in the world is the availability of water. In the days before tap water the nearer a house was to water the better. Our forefathers daily task of carrying water to the home from springs, brooks, lakes or pools was not only tiring but time consuming.

If houses were built quite far from a water supply or if the local brook was liable to run dry or be polluted by livestock, people dug wells. Sometimes the wells did not have to be dug very deep before water was reached, in other places they were quite a depth.

As with any task, certain people became very experienced at sinking wells, which was a dangerous job, often taken on by ex-miners. Well-diggers were in constant demand to keep the rapidly expanding population supplied with adequate water.

At a time when Liverpool was expanding rapidly, the 1769 "Liverpool Directory", records *"That the method of supplying water to the town at this time was the ancient one of each street sinking its own well"*. When the number of streets was rapidly increasing the well-sinker would be an important man. In 1769 the Liverpool well-sinker and miner was one James Lord of Moor Street.

The following century Wirral experienced a population explosion similar to that of Liverpool's. During the middle of the last century the Mersey bank of the peninsula became industrialised and many East Wirral villages grew into towns in a matter of decades. For instance the population of Birkenhead rose from just 200 in 1821 to 24,285 in 1851, in the same period Oxton's population grew from 165 to 2,007, Tranmere from 825 to 6,519, Lower Bebington from 316 to 1,492, Higher Bebington from 216 to 1,478, Liscard from 347 to 4,100, and Seacombe from 380 to 3,044. All these new residents needed a regular water supply.

Villages in North and West Wirral also grew at an alarming rate when the railway network spread from the 1860s to the 1890s and linked them to Wallasey, Birkenhead and Liverpool. During this period the populations of Neston, Heswall, West Kirby, Hoylake and Meols also grew rapidly.

All this increase in population made a great demand on water supplies. In the more built up areas each street had its own well. In the village areas one or two wells were sunk to supply new rows of cottages but farms and big houses had their own private wells.

In places like Heswall wells were especially important as there was very little running water. Considering the size of the Heswall area, (Heswall 1,149 acres, Oldfield 171 acres and Gayton 700 acres) there is a distinct lack of brooks which must be due to the porous sandstone rock soaking up the rainfall. Heswall is said to have taken its name from a well close to where Vikings established a settlement. The well situated on a hillside near hazel trees was called "Hazel Well" in a lane called Well Rake. According to local folklore, the "Hazel Well" became known as the "Hessle Well" which gave its name to Heswall. "Rake" is a Norse word for a narrow sloping lane which cattle were driven down to pasture. Well Rake became the steep lane now known as Wall Rake. Many villages in Wirral have sloping lanes or roads called "Rakes".

The wells in Gayton and Heswall were very old and most had old names such as "Far Well" in Well Lane, "Wishing Well" in Gayton Farm Road, "Hessle Well" in Wall Rake, "Prense Well" between the Puddy Dale and Heswall Cross, and "Piper Well" below Oldfield, which gave its name to Pipers Lane.

In the 1860s the Heswall well-sinker was Samuel Taylor from Neston and in the same period in Neston, wells were being sunk by Samuel Matthews from Bollington.

Wells were not just sunk anywhere. Convenience, the presence of water and being in a spot which would not become polluted for one reason or another, were all important factors to be considered before work began. From ancient times people were careful not to get their water supply from below graveyards. Years ago all bodies were buried and not cremated, so water used from an area close to a graveyard but on lower ground would almost certainly be polluted.

When sinking a well in soil or clay the biggest worry was that it might cave in. The well-sinker started by digging a circular hole a couple of feet deep often to about six feet in diameter. He then placed a sturdy iron ring in the hole and built a wall of bricks on top of it up to ground level. Then the earth under the ring was dug away, undermining it. The ring, with the weight of the wall of bricks on it, slid further down the hole. The well-sinker's mate then laid another couple of layers of bricks on top and gradually the well was lined with a circular brick wall. The iron ring would be undermined again allowing it to slide deeper down and more bricks were built on top. Many-a-time iron rings were not available and bricks were laid onto the bare clay, then carefully undermined.

When the depth of the proposed well got to about eight feet the well-sinker shovelled the clay into a bucket or basket which his mate hauled up on a rope pully fixed to a tripod and tipped it into a cart ready for transporting away. When water was found the last layers of brick were built up to about three feet above ground level to stop animals and children from falling down. The sinker was then gradually lowered down the well on a cradle with a bucket of mortar, a hammer and a trowel to tidy up the brick lining called the "steening", which comes from the old English "staenan" meaning stone. The final job was to build a hand-operated winch to wind a rope around for drawing buckets of water from the well.

Sinking a well. As the brick lining was undermined it slid down and more bricks were laid on top.

In the late Victorian era wells were often capped with slabs of sandstone which had holes bored through them. A long lead suction pipe, with a plunger fitted in the bore, was then lowered down into the water. At the top of the pipe a hand pump was fitted which was snugly located in the stone well cap. By using the handle to pump the plunger up and down, a vacuum was created which drew the water from the well up the lead pipe and out through the spout. On old maps P for pump indicated a well with a pump and a W shows the location of an open well where a bucket was used.

In areas like Heswall, Thurstaston, Caldy and Bidston where there is a lot of solid rock, sinking a well was particularly hard work but reasonably safe as the sides rarely caved in. The well-sinker cleared away any loose soil and exposed the solid rock at the chosen position. He then lit a good fire on the rock. When the rock was very hot it was dowsed with buckets of cold water. This caused the rock to crack. The well sinker could then hammer wedges into the cracks and break up the rock and clear it away. Then another fire was lit in the hole and the rock dowsed again. Gradually a well was sunk and the bore diameter was tidied up with a hammer and chisel. The well-sinker's mate would draw the rock up out of the well using his bucket and tripod. When water was reached, the well sinker tidied up the bottom of the well and either climbed out using the rope or was hauled out.

The rock excavated when sinking a well was used to improve roads. Even in areas of solid clay, granite stones dug up were useful for cobbling farmyards and filling in ruts in cart tracks etc. Most old farms in Wirral have cobbled yards of granite duck stones from wells and ploughed fields.

There have been a number of deaths due to people falling down wells for one reason or another. An entry in Heswall Church records for January 1803 records the son of Catherine Glover being found drowned in Gayton well. Gayton well, often referred to as the wishing well, has been capped for many years and can still be seen in the left bank of Gayton Farm Road off Well Lane.

From being a very important job, particularly during the population explosions of Victorian days, suddenly well-sinkers were redundant. Around the turn of the century fresh water was piped into most areas. Some isolated cottages in Ness, Heswall, Barnston and other villages had to rely on wells for another 10 or 20 years until the West Cheshire Water Board could find time for their gangs of navvies to dig long trenches and lay new water pipes to them.

Every now and again an old well is discovered somewhere, usually when building work is carried out. When my dad was a young lad before the Great War, his father had some tarmacadam dropped off to level ruts in his small farmyard in Holm Lane. Outside the shippen was a small round hole into which he tipped a whole bucket and then another. So he decided to investigate and got a big hammer and began to loosen up some of the big stones around the hole. As he walked away to get a pinch bar to lever them up there was a rumble and he looked round to see the ground fall away and a gaping hole appear, which turned out to be an old well. To find out how deep the well was, Grandad tied a brick to a cart-rope and lowered it down. He used the whole length of rope to reach the bottom.

The farm was owned by the Earl of Shrewsbury and his estate office was informed of the well. One of the estate employees was sent round to make things safe. Plumber Jimmy Egan of Woodchurch Lane arrived (the brother of Billy Egan who became Mayor of Birkenhead). Jimmy cleared all the big stones from around the top of the well, put irons across the hole and heavy boards on top. He then mixed concrete and capped the well with a foot-thick slab which Grandad tarmaced over. The well is probably still there.

THREE WIRRAL HILLS

Wirral is not a hilly area although ridges run down each side of the peninsula. Toward the Mersey we have a long ridge running from Bebington through Prenton, Tranmere and Oxton to Bidston. Another ridge runs parallel with the Dee through the Heswall, Pensby, Thurstaston and Caldy areas to Grange, West Kirby.

All the hills have names but are really quite small, some such as Bidston Hill appear to be higher than they are because they rise steeply from the docks at sea level and low lying land slightly above sea level.

It is a gradual climb from the River Dee to Heswall, then the ground levels out a bit and rises again to the top of Heswall Hill at Poll Hill Road and Tower Road North. The climb is one mile and it doesn't seem to be so high until you stand on top and look around. It can be deceiving, but Heswall Hill is the highest point in Wirral at 350 feet above sea level, but it is by no means the steepest.

Some of the best known hills and their heights above sea level are Thurstaston Hill 298, Caldy 250, Bidston 216, Ford 185, and Grange Hill 179. Most hills take their names from the village where they are situated, others are Arrowe Hill, Thingwall Hill, Irby Hill, Upton Hill and Prenton Hill.

There are many other hills, some quite well known and others with local names hardly known outside the area where they are. Some of these local names are taken from the roads which go up them, or old buildings, pubs and other landmarks near by, examples are Bull Hill in Little Neston, Clay Hill in Neston, Windle Hill near Hinderton, The Beacons and School Hill in Heswall; Cross Hill, Thingwall; Montgomery Hill, Frankby; Black Horse Hill, West Kirby; Rest Hill, Storeton; Swan Hill, Prenton; Holt Hill, Tranmere; Dacre Hill, Rock Ferry and St. Hilary Brow, Wallasey.

Some of the names are ancient. Cross Hill is said to be where the Vikings met to hold their parliament and its name also tells us it was probably some kind of religious meeting place. Holt Hill more than likely took the name from an old Anglo-Saxon word "holt", meaning a wood and The Beacons or Beacon Hill was one of a chain of hills where beacon fires stood ready to be lit as a warning of invasion.

Other hill names in Wirral are dying out such as The Plantin from Pensby up to Heswall which should properly be called The Plantation after the wood planted along the road near the top. Also Horrocks Hill from Harrocks Wood up to Irby and Chapel Hill from Moreton Cross up Hoylake Road, where an ancient Chapel once stood roughly where Digg Lane is.

Three ancient hill names which sadly are almost dead, are Bunkers Hill in Upton, Scarbrook Hill in Heswall and The Yeth at Woodchurch.

Bunkers Hill is the section of Arrowe Park Road running up from Upton Police Station to the cottages opposite Champion Spark Plugs. Arrowe House Farm, once the home of retired slave-ship owner and Lord Mayor of Liverpool, John Shaw, stood where Champions is and there were also two very old cottages a bit lower down. I have been brought up to know this part of Arrowe Hill as Bunkers Hill by my Dad and other older locals who always used this old name.

In Victorian days the name Bunkers Hill was actually the official address of the old cottages and shops most of which still stand there, this is plain to see on census records of Upton. The name "Bunker" is an old word meaning a large bank by the roadside, which there may well have been centuries ago. Out of habit, I still refer to this area as Bunkers Hill when giving directions or talking about the place, but most people look at me soft. I suppose I'll have to start describing it the modern way like most people and say "the hill next to Champions".

Old cottages at the top of Bunkers Hill opposite Champion Spark Plugs.

Some of the older locals in Heswall still call the hill up Delavor Road, The Scabbrick. Actually the name was Scarbrook Hill after the brook which ran down it before the days of culverts. The brook was so named because it cut a scar in the red sandstone. Owing to the local dialect spoken years ago it became known as Scabbrook Road in Victorian days.

However when I asked old locals why they called the hill The Scabbrick they all told me the same tale, which was that when they were children going to Heswall Shore down what is now Delavor Road, the road was steep and unmade. It was covered in ruts and potholes, some half filled with loose stones and bricks. They said that they always tripped over the stone and bricks either going up from, or down to, the shore and grazed their knees which resulted in them having scabby legs. So locals called the hill The Scabbrick. It just shows how names change over the years.

A couple of years ago retired farm worker Harold Candeland from Pensby asked me if I had mentioned The Yeth in any of my writings. I looked at him a bit soft as he had one on me, it was a name I had never heard and I thought I knew a bit about the local area. Harold explained that when he was a lad living in Landican where his dad worked on Okell's farm, the old local name for the hill up Woodchurch Road from what is now Ackers Road to Arrowe Park roundabout, was called The Yeth.

A day or two later I went to visit my two "walking local history books" - my Dad who was then 90 and farmer George Bowden who is the same age. I had a few questions to ask. Both agreed with what Harold had told me. The hill up to the roundabout was commonly known as The Yeth, mainly in the farming communities of Landican and Woodchurch up until the 1920s. Evidently my uncle Chuck Wilbraham who lived in Landican where his father was a farm bailiff before the Great War, always called this hill, The Yethy Hill. My dad and George both said that it was years since they had heard the old name which more or less went out of circulation when they were young.

Looking down Delavor Road towards Heswall Shore from what was once known as Scarbrook Hill.

With a bit of research I got to the bottom of the old name "Yeth" which is an old dialect word meaning "heathland". Therefore land covered in gorse and heather which years ago would usually be rough common land. Woodchurch Common once stretched across this hill and is clearly marked on old maps. Before the Woodchurch Estate was built the name of the field on the hill was the "Common Field". I believe it was always rough and even today you can see sandstone rock sticking out from the grass verge between Woodchurch Road and Common Field Road.

So The Yeth or The Yethy Hill had an accurate meaning as do most old place names if you can only dig the information out. Finding out what these old hill names mean is no "big deal", but unfortunately our older friends and relations will not always be here to help and if details are not recorded then they are lost. Who knows, somebody in years to come might be researching their family and find these names on old documents or letters and wonder where they are. Now they will have something to refer to.

Looking across the cornfield at Woodchurch Road. This hill was once known as the Yeth. The houses of Common Field Road, Woodchurch can be seen stretching towards Arrowe Park roundabout.

WIRRAL'S OLYMPIC MARATHON RUNNER

The origin of the Marathon race and its unusual length goes back to 490 B.C. when the Persians invaded Greece. Greek city states had helped Ionia rebel against Persian rule so King Darius of Persia decided to punish them. He sent messengers to the major Greek cities demanding that they surrender. Most cities did but some refused including Athens, Sparta, Plataea and Eretria. The messengers sent to Athens were imprisoned and those sent to Sparta were thrown down a well.

The Persian invasion fleet was sent to the island city of Eretria which it besieged and destroyed before sailing to attack Athens. The famous Athenian long-distance runner Pheidippides was sent to Sparta to ask for help. Pheidippides was a professional runner which means he earned his living as a kind of postman delivering messages over long distances from city to city. He ran 156 miles from Athens to Sparta over rough country, climbing mountains and swimming rivers and was said to have arrived the next day. When he reached Sparta he found the city in the middle of a religious festival and was told that no help could be sent until the moon was full. Pheidippides then ran back to Athens with the bad news.

The Athenians, with some allies from Plataea, decided to march out of the city and fight the Persians rather than wait and be besieged. The two armies met at a place near the sea called Marathon. The Athenians were out-numbered two to one but they were on high ground. They charged downhill at full speed into the Persian ranks which held in the centre but gave way at the flanks. The Athenian flanks then turned on the Persian centre from both sides and won a great victory. The Persians retreated to their ships and escaped but they left over 6,000 dead. Athenian losses were only 192 and an unknown number of Plataeans were killed.

Pheidippides fought in the battle, then ran slightly over 26 miles along rough tracks from Marathon to Athens with the good news. When he reached Athens he called, "rejoice, we conquer", but his exhausting days of continual hard running and fighting proved too much for him and he collapsed and died.

The modern Olympic Games were resurrected by Frenchman, Baron Pierre de Coubertin in 1896. They were held in Athens where 60,000 enthusiastic spectators packed the stadium and thousands more watched from the surrounding hills. In honour of Pheidippides, a race was run from Marathon to Athens which was then 24 miles, probably due to roads being improved and straightened. A Greek shepherd called Spyridon Louis won the race and his fellow Greeks were ecstatic, women even threw jewellery to him. As Louis neared the winning post Prince George and Crown Prince Constantine of Greece hurried down from their seats bursting with pride and ran the last few yards either side of him. Another Greek was second and a Hungarian was third. These were the first Games held in Greece since the ancient games at Olympia were abolished by the Christian Emperor Theodosius I in A.D. 393.

The Games proved a success and from then on were held every four years in a different country. In 1908 the Olympic Games were held in London. The Marathon race which started at Windsor Park was set at 26 miles 385 yards so that it finished in front of the royal box in White City Stadium. At the 1912 Olympics in Stockholm the Marathon was altered to 25 miles but in 1924 the Olympic Marathon was re-set at 26 miles 385 yards which it is today.

Every year there is also an international race to commemorate Pheidippides' 156 mile run from Athens to Sparta. A local man from Greasby, Alan Tomkinson, has competed in this long-distance run, but the record holder is amateur Greek runner and taxi driver Yanis Kouros who completed the run in an unbelievable 20 hours 25 minutes. The women's record is held by German, Helga Backhaus with a time of 29 hours 33 minutes.

As far as I know the only person from Wirral ever to represent Great Britain in the Olympic Games Marathon was Septimus Francom of Thingwall. Seppy, as he was better known, came from a Liverpool family who moved to Wirral. His father Joseph Francom was a plumber and painter from Mann Island in Liverpool. In 1870 Joseph brought his wife Mary and their four children over the Mersey to live in Upton, Wirral in one of the cottages which still stand opposite Champion Spark Plugs, between "The Stirrup" pub and Woodland Road, an area then known as Bunkers Hill.

In 1880 Joseph Francom and family moved from Upton into a newly built semi-detached sandstone cottage in Thingwall called "Heather Villa", situated in a quiet lane now called Holmwood Drive. Mr. and Mrs. Francom's family had grown considerably by then, they had seven children living at home and their two eldest, 19 year old Mary Esther and Josiah aged 17 were living and working elsewhere. Josiah was not far away at "Thingwall Hall" coach house where he was employed as a groom.

The Francom's next door neighbours were the Newton family who lived in the adjoining semi-detached called "Pinnington". Thomas Newton was a farm labourer from West Kirby. Usually semi-detached houses have a dividing wall from front to back, but "Heather Villa" and "Pinnington" were divided through the middle from left to right, from gable end to gable end. Therefore one semi was entered from the front and the other round the back. In those days the only other house in the lane was "Common Farm" run by the Brown family. At the turn of the century this farm was abandoned and became derelict. The lane then became known as Francom's Lane before it was officially called Holmwood Drive.

The Francom's tenth child was born in their new home, "Heather Villa" and baptised at Woodchurch Church on 30th April 1882. The baby boy was their seventh son and they christened him Septimus, which is Latin meaning "seventh born". He grew into a tall lad and as a schoolboy it became obvious that Seppy was a gifted runner. He left school in the 1890s starting work as a labourer on the laying of the New Brighton to Wrexham Railway and ran to and from work as part of the training for his hobby of long distance running.

There was not much organised running in Wirral in the 1890s so Seppy joined Richmond Club in Liverpool and then Sefton Harriers where he became a member of their marathon team which won the Hackenschmidt Trophy against all comers in 1900-1901.

At this time he was courting Sarah Ann Parr, the daughter of James Parr, a Heswall-born farm labourer who lived and worked on the Arrowe Estate before it became Arrowe Park. Seppy and Sarah Ann were married at Woodchurch Church in 1901 when they were both only 19 years old. One of the witnesses was his friend Enoch Roberts, the Pensby Blacksmith.

In 1902 Sarah Ann gave birth to Arthur, the first of their six children. About this time Seppy became involved in racing pigeons, a hobby which was to remain one of his main interests throughout his life. He was by now known far and wide as a very powerful and well respected runner. In 1905 at the age of 23 Seppy became the Captain of Sefton Harriers and kept up his training of running to work for the Railway where he was then employed as a platelayer.

Also in 1905 Prenton Golf Club was formed and in about 1908 Seppy left his job with the Railway to become the first full time greenkeeper at the Prenton course. He was very happy in his new job as not only did he prefer the type of work but he was also involved with sport.

On 11th May 1911 Wirral Athletic Club was formed and Seppy was a founder member. He was held in high regard both as a man and as a runner and on 18th September 1911 he was elected onto the committee. Seppy's running ability was by this time well known in sporting circles throughout the country. On 2nd March 1912 he won the Liverpool and District Cross Country Title and also in the same year he won the Hull Marathon. During the running season of October 1911 to March 1912 he put a number of important wins under his belt and set his sights on his dream of competing in the 1912 Olympic Games. He hammered home this claim by finishing 4th in a race used for the Olympic Marathon trial. Seppy was the second Briton home and was chosen to represent Great Britain at the Games in Stockholm.

Prenton Golf Club gave him 14 days leave of absence and on Saturday 30th June 1912, Seppy left the country for Sweden. A week before the race a severe and prolonged heatwave hit Stockholm and temperatures rose to 90 degrees Fahrenheit. Athletics teams, including the British asked for the marathon to be postponed but the Officials refused to change the schedule. According to the "Birkenhead News" of Saturday 20 July 1912 the race started at 1.50 pm. on Monday from Stockholm with 69 competitors.

The chosen time could not have been worse during a heat wave, the men had to run the 25 miles through the sweltering afternoon heat. Many runners wore handkerchiefs and hats to save their heads from the scorching sun.

The race began at a fast pace and as the heat of the day intensified and the miles wore on, runners began to drop out. Tatu Kolehmainen (Finland) and Gitsham (South Africa) went into the lead with Speroni (Spain) and local favourite Jacobsson (Sweden) close behind. About halfway round, Gitsham, still at the front was joined by his fellow countryman McArthur. The gruelling pace and wilting heat was now causing more competitors to retire. Even Kolehmainen, one of the favourites dropped out exhausted and so did Great Britain's representative, our own Septimus Francom. The 21 year old Portuguese runner Francisco Lazaro collapsed at somewhere between 19 and 22 miles and later died from a combination of sunstroke and heart trouble. Approaching the stadium Gitsham paused for a drink and the big powerful dark haired Ken McArthur seized the opportunity to take the lead and go on to win. Only 34 of the 69 runners finished.

The first six and their times were as follows; first Kennedy Kane McArthur (South Africa 2hrs. 36min. 54sec.), second Christian W. Gitsham (South Africa 2:37:52), third Gaston Strobino (U.S.A. 2:38:42), fourth Andrew Sockalexis (U.S.A. 2:42:08), fifth James Duffy (Canada 2:42:19) and 6th Sigfrid Jacobsson (Sweden 2:43:25).

Although Ken McArthur represented South Africa he was actually born in the village of Dervock, County Antrim, Northern Ireland where he worked as a postman. At the age of 24 he emigrated to South Africa and became a policeman in the Transvaal. When interviewed by reporters after the race he told them "I went out to win or die". Ken McArthur is still the only British-born runner to win the Olympic Marathon. Another British-born athlete who won a gold medal at Stockholm was Englishman George Goulding, representing Canada in the 10,000 metres walk. Ken McArthur and Seppy were both 31 years old when they competed at the 1912 Stockholm Olympics.

The 1912 Olympics were the best to date and provided some exceptional sporting achievements. During these Games, Finland, though competing under the Russian flag, emerged as an athletics power. Hannes Kolehmainen, brother of Tatu, became the first "flying Finn" and won the cross country, the 10,000 metres and the 5,000 metres, setting a new World record. But the star of the Games was an American of mixed Red Indian and Irish blood. His tribal name was "Bright Path" but he was known as Jim Thorpe. Thorpe won the pentathlon, beating amongst others, fellow American George S. Paton who later became the famous Second World War general. He also took the decathlon by a remarkable 680 points. When King Gustav of Sweden presented Thorpe with his medals he said "Sir, you are the greatest athlete in the world". Thorpe replied "Thanks, King". However it was later found out that years earlier Thorpe had accepted a very small amount of money for playing baseball. This brought into doubt his amateur status and in 1913 he was stripped of his medals, but the runners-up refused to accept them.

Back home in England in 1912, Seppy had the honour of being elected Senior Captain of Wirral A.C. After the disappointment at Stockholm he got back into his winning ways and in the following year won the Hull Marathon and the Liverpool and District Cross Country title again. In 1914 he won both these races yet again and also the West Lancashire Cross Country Championship. Having won the Hull Marathon three years running he was given the cup to keep.

During the Great War 1914-1918 all organised sport was suspended. Most of Prenton Golf Course was turned over to agriculture and used for grazing livestock. The course professional was given his notice and Seppy was sent to work at Cammell Lairds Shipyard.

After the War Seppy was re-employed at Prenton. Competitive running did not resume until 1920 when he again won the Liverpool and District Cross Country title. In the following year he and his 19 year old son Arthur both ran in this event and remarkably finished 1st and 2nd. The next year (1923) Seppy at the age of 42 was beaten in the Liverpool and District C.C. race for the first time since he won it in 1912.

As time went on he was blessed with grandchildren and family photographs were taken with the babies in the big Hull Marathon Cup. I believe Seppy was by now head greenkeeper at Prenton Golf Club and had more or less retired from running by the late 1920s. But he had other hobbies to spend his spare time on being a very successful pigeon fancier. Over the years his pigeons won most of the big races from the continent and he also travelled throughout the British Isles both showing and judging pigeons.

Seppy's best mate was Peter Roberts who lived not far away in "Quarry Cottage", Sparks Lane and worked as a blacksmith's striker at Tom Lee's foundry in Woodchurch. I knew Peter well, he shared the same interests as my Dad and Seppy, racing pigeons and rabbiting. Peter stood just over five feet and Seppy was a tall man. I believe they looked a rum pair when they went rabbiting together in their long coats, big boots and flat caps, Peter walking his big lurcher and Seppy carrying his ferrets.

Whilst working at the golf course during the 1920s he was sometimes plagued at weekends by gangs from Birkenhead. These lads mainly from the old Dock Cottages came to dredge the pits for golf balls. Seppy warned them off but there were often a dozen or more of them and they were hard faced and told him to go away. Seppy was a crack shot with a catapult and he would let the Birkenhead lads have it in the legs or backside with marbles. They would charge at him in a rage but being a fit runner he just loped away, turned and shot them again. The golf ball hunters soon got the message and moved on to safer ground.

During the 1930s Seppy employed his sons Arthur and Ben as assistant greenkeepers and Jack Smith of Sandy Lane, Heswall was greenkeeper and tractor driver.

When the Second World War started in 1939 Ben Francom was called up and eventually only Seppy and Jack remained at Prenton. One night during the blitz in May 1941, the Club House was bombed but luckily Seppy and other men serving as fire watchers managed to put the flames out.

During the war, Ben Francom, also a good runner, was captured by the Germans but escaped more than once by running away from working parties. To stop his gallop the Germans shot him in the foot. After the war was over, Ben Francom followed in his father's foot-steps and became head greenkeeper at Heswall Golf Course with Jack Smith's son Alan. Alan previously worked for his uncle Harry Shakeshaft, head greenkeeper at Wirral Ladies Golf Course where American troops had been camping.

I believe Septimus Francom was a hard task master and as enthusiastic and keen in his job as he was about his running and pigeon fancying. He remained as head greenkeeper until his retirement in 1947. Sadly, his wife Sarah Ann died in 1948.

Tractor driver Jack Smith (left) and Head Greenkeeper Seppy Francom (right) at Prenton Golf Course after a heavy snowfall c.1935.

My Dad and farmer George Bowden knew Seppy well. When he retired from the golf course he sometimes did a bit of farm work such as hedging, ditching, potato picking and helping out at harvest time. I think he liked the company and talking about old times. In those days the Prince family who were coal merchants lived next door to him in "Pinnington". As a lad one of my jobs in the late 1950s and early '60s, when most people had no telephone, was to run over the fields to Holmwood Drive and order coal for my Dad. In those days Holmwood Drive led to Thingwall Children's Sanatorium. Today Murrayfield BUPA Hospital stands on the site.

Septimus James Francom died on 15th March 1965, a year after his eldest son Arthur and was buried at Woodchurch Church with his wife Sarah Ann, son Arthur and daughter Amelia. His daughter Florence continued to live in "Heather Villa" through the 1970s and 80s. After she died the old cottage went out of the Francom name after over 100 years. "Heather Villa" and "Pinnington" were made into one house called "Heather Cottage" which was tastefully modernised and extended in 1993.

Men like Seppy are examples to today's athletes. They were true amateurs who could rarely afford to get, or got, time off work to train or run. Even Ken McArthur couldn't get time off from the Transvaal Police Force to run. They had no-one to advise or train them and devised their own methods, time tables and routines. Athletics was largely the sport of young gentlemen of means. Lads like Seppy had to train by running to and from work. They were often helped by friends or relations who paced them on push bikes. One of Seppy's own training methods was to run along the railway line to and from work and again for hours after work, stepping from sleeper to sleeper as he reckoned this was the best method to ensure equal strides. All trains were steam operated then so there was no fear of being electrocuted.

In those days there were no high calory special diets or extra money to pay for them. The working class athletes of Seppy's era probably had more guts and determination than many sportsmen today, even the shoes they wore would put some runners off. He gained great pleasure both from his work and his hobbies and was successful in his chosen fields, reaching the highest standards as a runner, pigeon fancier and greenkeeper.

INJUSTICE IN BIRKENHEAD

During the 1880s and '90s a number of respectable and hard working Austrian and German families emigrated to England for a better life. Quite a few settled in Liverpool, Wallasey and Birkenhead where some opened pork butchers' shops.

One such German immigrant was Karl Deuschle who was married at the German Chapel, Renshaw Street, Liverpool in 1892. Karl and his wife established their own business two years later, opening a pork butcher's shop at 35 Oxton Road, Birkenhead. They had three sons, Charles born in 1894, Frederick in 1897 and William in 1900.

Karl worked hard to build up his business. He bought his pigs live from local farmers, smallholders and cottagers who soon got to know him and found he was a very honest and likeable man. Karl, or Charley as they affectionately called him, became renowned for paying exactly what the pigs were worth and not haggling too much or trying to get one over on people. The instant a price was agreed, he paid up.

Cottagers were people who had a large garden or a couple of small crofts and kept a few pigs and hens etc., to add to their low wage as, say, a farm labourer or gardener. In Victorian days and during the early 1900s there were quite a few cottagers living on the rural outskirts of Birkenhead in such places as Oxton, Bidston, Prenton, Upton and Bebington. To these not-so-well-off people, the sale of a litter of pigs which they had been fattening up for months, made the difference between scraping by and being able to live a little bit more comfortably. The pig money usually rigged their children out in new clothes or maybe bought some much needed household items.

My grandparents had a seven acre smallholding in Holm Lane, Oxton and always sold their pigs to Karl as did their neighbours the Bennetts, Whartons and others. Karls business prospered and he opened another pork butcher's which was a lock-up shop, at 135 Price Street, Birkenhead.

Some time between 1900 and 1906 Karl changed his name from Karl Deuschle to Charles Dashley and applied for British citizenship for himself and his family, which was granted in 1911. His oath of allegiance to the Crown went as follows: I Karl Deuschle known as Charles Dashley of 35 Oxton Road etc. etc....

My dad, who was born in 1906 used to help his older brother and sisters drive pigs from Holm Lane to Charles' shop in Oxton Road via Rose Mount and Balls Road. There was no traffic in those days and livestock being driven along the roads was a common sight. Usually though, Charles or one of his sons arrived at granddads smallholding in a pony and float to pick up the pigs, especially if there was a big sow to be taken. The pig or pigs were loaded in the float and a net was thrown over the top and tied down so they couldn't jump out.

All was going well for Charles and his business until 1914 when the Great War started and his country of origin was fighting his adopted homeland. To his customers and suppliers the war made no difference in their attitude to Charles, he had lived here for years and was "part of the furniture".

Then on Friday 7th. May 1915 a dreadful thing happened, the Cunard Line ship "Lusitania" was sunk off Kinsale, Ireland by a torpedo fired from the German submarine U.20. by Lieutenant Walther Schwieger. Of the 1,959 passengers and crew aboard the "Lusitania" 1,195 perished including 123 Americans on their way to Liverpool. Many Merseyside families lost loved ones and there was obviously great anger and hatred of anything German. People could not get their hands on the U-Boat crew so they took it out on innocent Austrians and Germans living amongst them.

Thomas Evans on deck. Thomas was born in Parkgate and worked as a Dee fisherman in his younger days. In 1892 he married farmers daughter Alice Roberts of Hillside Farm, School Lane, Thurstaston and they lived in Marlfield Cottage, Pensby Road which had been built for Alice by her brothers in 1887. Thomas later went deep-sea with Cunard Line and eventually became Chief Quartermaster and Helmsman on the Lusitania and unfortunately lost his life when she was torpedoed in 1915. His granddaughter Valery Steel, her husband David and mother May still live in Marlfield Cottage which stands opposite the Esso Garage.

The day after the sinking of the "Lusitania" anti-German riots broke out in major British cities including Liverpool. German and Austrian owned shops, businesses and houses were attacked, looted and wrecked. Birkenhead Police and German shopkeepers were expecting the riots to spread "over the water", and pubs were advised to close early.

Sure enough, anti-German riots started in Birkenhead on the Monday night. The first victim was John Swarb who had his pork butcher's shop at 49 Watson Street wrecked. Police tried to protect the premises from the mob but they were stoned and overwhelmed by sheer numbers.

The next shops to be attacked were Charles Dashley's in Price Street and Oxton Road. Charles was expecting trouble and had sent his wife out of harm's way but he stayed in his home above the shop in Oxton Road. When the mob broke in he managed to give them the slip. Most of the rioters were looters who had no idea who the people were whose businesses they were attacking. Charles' grandson Fred Dashley of New Milton, Hants was told that his grandfather actually moved around his home amongst the mob, collecting small items of sentimental value and putting them in his pockets. The rioters ransacked and looted the Dashley home and shop below, throwing personal possessions and furniture through windows to the street below where they were set on fire. Some of the mob found Mr. Dashley's trap and pushed it down Oxton Road and made off with it.

Before anybody recognised him, Charles made good his escape and fled to Holm Lane were my Grandparents hid him for a while. They had family members fighting the Germans in France but they still stood by Charles and looked after him. My Grandparents had a large family and things were a bit cramped in their cottage so Charles was moved into a neighbour's house where there was more room. My dad was nine at the time and he recalls being told not to talk to anyone about what had gone on and he was not told where Charles was moved to.

The riots continued for a couple of days and pubs remained closed. About 20 odd Austrian and German businesses and houses in Birkenhead were attacked but in Liverpool the number was nearer 200. It was understandable up to a point as many Merseyside families had relatives serving in the crew of the "Lusitania", especially in Liverpool.

However, as could be expected, a great many of the rioters were only interested in looting whatever goods they could get their hands on. Some businesses had no connection with Germany but malicious rumours spread and they were looted. In Exmouth Street, a greengrocers belonging to Mrs. Jones, a very good-hearted lady who often did charity work, was looted and wrecked for no apparent reason. The shop and home of fried fish dealer Thomas Lincoln at 220 Price Street was also completely smashed up by the mob comprised mainly of young women and boys. They looted everything they could get their hands on and used tablecloths to carry off stolen goods. Mr. Lincoln's shop was attacked because someone said that he had sold fish to a German.

The people whose premises were attacked lost everything they had, as well as having their homes completely wrecked. Even some private houses were attacked such as the home of Mary Fuchs at 57 Bidston Avenue. The wrecked shops were boarded up and guarded by police. Pubs remained closed all week but there was no repetition of the riots and police got to work tracking down looters, rioters and people who had assaulted them. Some rioters were caught and fined, others were imprisoned for a short time.

Mr. and Mrs. Dashley went into hiding until things died down a bit and kept a low profile for the rest of the war.

The bitter injustice that many Germans suffered was that even though many had sons fighting for Great Britain they were still targeted. Even worse, many had lived in Liverpool and Birkenhead for decades and their children were English-born, but unfortunately they had not applied for British citizenship. This resulted in them being interned in camps in the Isle of Man until the end of the war when they were banished to Germany with their English children. How wrong and unjust this was.

Charles Dashley's three sons all served with distinction in the Great War. Charles junior was already in the Merchant Navy when war was declared. He first went to sea in 1908 at only 14 years of age aboard the sailing vessel "Carmenian". Charles served throughout the four years of conflict on a number of ships. He was Second Mate on the "Glen Carron" when it was torpedoed in the English Channel. Luckily he survived to carry on his service aboard another vessel.

Some of the shops hit by the Birkenhead Riots in 1915.

Charles Dashley's pork butchers shop in Oxton Road, boarded up after being wrecked by rioters.

Frederick (Fred) served with the 2nd Manchesters 9th battalion in France. He was twice wounded, once during the Passchendaele Campaign in October 1917 and again in March 1918 when his battalion was sent to stem the German advance on the Fifth Army positions. After the war ended Fred returned to the family butchery business.

William (Bill) the youngest son, a former pupil of the Woodlands School and Birkenhead Institute, joined the Merchant Navy as a cadet and sailed aboard the British steamship "Governor". In March 1917 the notorious German raider "Moewe" attacked and sank the "Governor" killing four crewmen and wounding 10 including 16 year old Bill who was hit by gunfire. After this encounter Bill was taken to Germany where he remained as a prisoner of war until hostilities ended 21 months later.

After the war ended the lock-up shop in Price Street remained closed but Charles re-opened his Oxton Road shop and my grandparents and his other old friends carried on doing business with him and his family as before. Most people realised it was no fault of Charles Dashley that they had lost loved ones although understandably many people were bitter.

Bill Dashley remained at sea when the war ended and in 1921 took his Second Mate's ticket. Eventually he left the Merchant Navy and re-joined the family business in Oxton Road. From 1922 and into the 1930s my grandparents were farming at Gallopers Lane, Thingwall and continued to supply Charles and his sons Bill and Fred with pigs. In 1932 Charles Dashley, the well respected pork butcher, died and Bill then managed the family business on behalf of his mother. Unfortunately the Dashley family suffered a further loss when Fred died in 1934.

When the Second World War started Bill Dashley volunteered for the Merchant Navy reserve. As at the start of the Great War, Charles junior was already at sea when war was declared in 1939. Now the Captain of the "City of Mobile", he was involved, along with a number of both Merchant and Royal Navy ships in the rescue of Allied troops and civilians from St. Nazaire, France in June 1940. During this operation he rescued thousands of soldiers but his ship was hit, so he got her under way and manoeuvred about so as to make a more difficult target for the German bombers.

However the Cunard Line ship "Lancastria" commanded by Captain R. Sharp of Wallasey, with 9,000 troops and civilians aboard remained at anchor to wait for an escort. She received several direct hits from German aircraft. A bomb dropped in No. 2 hatch where about 1,000 Air Force men were packed in the lower hold. Another wave of German aircraft attacked and she was again hit, this time on the foredeck and a bomb also dropped down the funnel. Several other British ships were also hit. As the "Lancastria" went down, oil from her bunker tanks spread across the water where thousands of survivors, including women and children, were swimming for their lives. The German 'planes returned to machine gun survivors and drop incendiary bombs to try and ignite the oil slick. Fortunately Royal Air Force Spitfires came to the rescue and scattered the German aircraft.

British ships then risked their own destruction to rescue survivors but a French tug was seen to manoeuvre through the wreckage, ignoring those drowning, and proceed on its way. Captain Dashley, already with 3,500 troops aboard, managed to rescue 50 survivors from the "Lancastria" and other British ships rescued thousands more.

Unfortunately, 3,000 lives were lost when the "Lancastria" went down, more than the combined losses of the "Lusitania" (1,195) and the "Titanic" (1,517). The sinking of the "Lancastria" was one of the greatest maritime disasters in British history, yet it is rarely mentioned.

Not long after the rescue at St. Nazaire, the "City of Mobile" was sunk by enemy aircraft in the Irish Sea between Belfast and Liverpool but luckily Captain Charles Dashley survived yet again. He was further involved in the evacuation of Allied troops from Crete and the Middle

East amongst other operations. For his distinguished war service Captain Dashley received the O.B.E. in 1942 from the King at Buckingham Palace.

As a boy in Birkenhead he was educated at The Woodlands and then at the Higher Elementary School in Conway Street. During his lifetime at sea, Captain Dashley became a member of the South African Master Mariners Association, a member of the Mercantile Marine Service Association and the Distinguished Company of Cape Horners (British Section). He and his wife lived at 73 Canning Street, Liverpool until he died at Sefton General Hospital in 1961 aged 68.

On the death of his mother, Bill inherited the family butchery business at 35 Oxton Road, which he ran until he died in 1979. Shortly after, the shop closed and 85 years of trading in Birkenhead by the honest and patriotic Dashley family came to an end.

Oddly, the two worst single maritime disasters of both World Wars touched the Dashley family. Because of the sinking of the "Lusitania", Britain's worst maritime disaster of the First World War, Charles Dashley and his wife suffered injustice and persecution. Yet because of the brave action of their son Charles Dashley junior, 50 lives were saved from the "Lancastria", Britain's worst maritime disaster of the Second World War. Both these Cunard Liners were built on the Clyde.

Some German and Austrian families living in Britain suffered more than one injustice as well as inhuman persecution. Having been rounded up during the First World War and interned on the Isle of Man as enemy aliens, some were exchanged for British non-combatants living in Germany. The rest were deported when the war ended in 1918, along with their English-born children. A number of these Germans were descended from Jewish families and having suffered at British hands, they were persecuted yet again in their homeland when Hitler came to power in 1933. After suffering years of persecution at the hands of the Nazis, some were tortured and murdered in concentration camps during the Second World War.

A WARTIME FISHERMAN

In Victorian days the fishing industry on the Dee coast of Wirral was in the hands of a close knit community. It was kept in a number of local family names and boats were handed down from father to son. Practically every fishing family went back in the local area for generations, apart from a couple of families in Heswall, namely James Rigby and son, shrimp fishermen from Southport and John Buckley and son, salmon fishermen from Handbridge in Chester.

By the 1930s the Dee was very seriously silted up and the fishing industry in Wirral was in decline. In the late 1930s there were only about a dozen Parkgate boats, or 'nobbies' as they were called, operated by the following eight families, Bushell, Campion, Cross, Fewtrell, Higgins, Mealor, Peters and Smith. At Heswall there was a small fleet operated by two remaining families, Lewis and Evans. The decline had come in less than a lifetime, 40 odd years earlier there were 73 fishermen living in the Heswall, Neston and Parkgate areas. (Nobbies are fishing boats with both sail and engine).

A couple of fishing families, Bedson and Slack, still operated out of the Mersey. They included Eaton Bedson of 84 Russell Road, Rock Ferry, Henry of 32 Sutton Road, New Brighton and William of 1 Balmoral Road, New Brighton. John Slack lived at 33 Ebenezer Street, Rock Ferry, Thomas at 48 Hinderton Road, Tranmere and Thomas Joseph Slack at 67 Lucania Street, Garston, Liverpool.

Ciggy Wakelam was not originally from the Heswall area or from a fishing family but he became one of the very few "outsiders" to become a full time Dee fisherman. This came about when his family moved to Heswall due to a series of events.

His father, Gerry, attended Woodchurch Road School where his exceptional footballing talent was highlighted and he became a schoolboy international winning four international caps. When he left school he went to work at Cammell Lairds and served an apprenticeship as a boilermaker. At the outbreak of war in 1914, Gerry joined the Cheshire Regiment as a Physical Training Instructor and served as a corporal in Ismailia, the Dardanelles and the Middle East.

After the war he became a professional footballer and played for Burnley where, in 1920, he injured his ankle. In those days footballers received no sick pay so he slung his boots over the railway railings and went back to Lairds to work at his trade for a guaranteed wage. Gerry left Lairds in about 1926 to work for Flemmings of Neston, constructing the Sunray Ward at Leasowe Hospital. To be near his job, he moved from his home in Hughes Lane, Oxton to a house at the bottom end of Pasture Road, close to Moreton shore.

When his firm went slack due to the hospital contract's completion, Mr. Flemming found Gerry a job as groundsman at Heswall Golf Club where he was captain. For convenience, Gerry and his family eventually moved to Mostyn Avenue near Heswall Shore at Christmastime 1928 when Ciggy was only three and a half years old. The houses in Mostyn Avenue were built the previous year by Jones and Hough of Heswall and were the first houses in Heswall to be built with breeze blocks.

Ciggy grew up in the rural fishing community known locally as "The Bonks" which included Mostyn Avenue, Banks Road and The Moorings. When he left school in 1938 Ciggy became a fisherman working with his mate Jacky Evans for Jacky's dad, old Bill. Bill Evans' Conway built nobby was called the "Polly" and they trawled for fish and shrimps in the Dee Estuary and off the Point of Ayr.

In some places the River Dee undermined the bank on the Welsh side and when cattle came to the edge, the bank sometimes carried away resulting in animals being drowned. The rotted carcasses of these cattle were sometimes trawled up in fishing nets. They were full of shrimps which Ciggy and the Evans' shook out onto the deck, then threw the carcass back for another lucky day.

Most of the fish were taken to Liverpool Market by fish dealer Jinny Sissons of Hinderton who was an Evans before marriage. Some of the catch was also sold to Heswall fishmongers Tarbucks, Drews and Redferns the grocers. Daniel Redfern also bought fish for his shops at 252-254 Old Chester Road, Tranmere and 369 Borough Road. Neston hawkers also bought smaller quantities of fish and shellfish which they took to sell in other areas.

Ciggy Wakelam, when he was a young fit 17 year old Heswall fisherman, standing in the back door-way of his house at 25 Mostyn Avenue.

At Heswall Golf Course, Joe Collins the course Professional went to serve in the Army and Gerry Wakelam, Ciggy's dad, took over his duties as well as being promoted to Head Groundsman when Bill Munnerly of Neston retired.

When the Second World War started in 1939 all young men from the fishing families of Wirral either volunteered or were called up to serve in the Navy. This left only lads like 15 year old Ciggy and older men to run the local fishing industry. Because so much allied shipping was torpedoed, food was rationed, so fishermen were instructed by the government to concentrate on catching fish to provide wholesome meals, rather than the delicacies of shrimps. Some old fishermen such as Jack "Up It" Evans came out of retirement to help the war effort.

One sunny morning shortly before dinner Ciggy, Jack and Bill were out fishing in "The Deep" off Mostyn when a "dog fight" started over Birkenhead and Liverpool between British and German aircraft. The fishermen watched as Spitfires and Messerschmitts chased each other across the sky. Some of the aircraft flew over the River Dee and suddenly a German fighter nose-dived straight for the "Polly" and strafed her. A line of bullets splashed into the water either side of the small boat and two hit her going right through the gunnels. Lucky enough no-one was hit. The German 'plane straightened up and headed for home pursued by a Spitfire which was reckoned to have shot it down over Denbighshire.

Some time later Jacky Evans went to serve King and country. Jacky didn't have to go as all his brothers were serving in the Navy and one son of a big family could be excused military service, but he wanted to "do his bit". His first taste of active service was as Royal Navy gunner seconded to a merchant ship.

Bill Evans' Heswall nobby the "Polly". Left to right, Ciggy Wakelam, Jack Evans and Bill Evans fishing Mostyn Deep in the River Dee.

Young Ciggy Wakelam, old Bill Evans and sometimes Jack "Up It" Evans were left to man the "Polly" and fish long hours, bringing in good catches for the war effort. Now and again they saw bodies floating out at sea, sometimes in rough weather, but old Bill went out of his way to recover them saying, "we'll get the lad home, he's some mothers son".

In 1942 Ciggy followed in the footsteps of all the other young fishermen from Heswall, Neston, Parkgate, Hoylake and elsewhere in the country and was called up to serve in the Royal Navy. He was first of all sent to Skegness and then to Plymouth for training. Eventually Ciggy was selected for service as a submariner and sent to Holy Loch submarine base at Dunoon, Scotland.

What an extreme and dangerous change in fortunes this was for a young country lad to cope with. To be one minute living at home and working out in the open air, then suddenly sent under the sea in a submarine to engage the enemy. Ciggy sailed out on active service in the submarine "Titania" which he served aboard until the Germans surrendered on 8th May 1945.

The war against the Japanese was still being fought in the Far East and Ciggy was sent to Plymouth to join the "Devonshire" bound for Singapore. He was Coxswain but was then acting Petty Officer when he met Jacky Evans again aboard the "Devonshire" in a working party. Ciggy looked after Jacky and Jacky returned the favours when he received a welcome envelope from Heswall. Jacky's dad, old Bill, had somehow acquired a book of railway warrants from the Akbar Nautical School in Heswall. Ciggy got the warrants stamped and they made a packet selling them at £1.00 to Liverpool and £1. 10 shillings (£1.50) to Glasgow. They had a whale of a time in the Plymouth pubs before Ciggy sailed for Singapore aboard the "Devonshire".

After arriving at Singapore Ciggy went ashore and bumped into two Heswall lads, Ronny McGeachin and Les Pover. They were a sight for sore eyes to Ciggy and they had a good old chin-wag. He was still at Singapore when Japan surrendered on 14th August 1945. Ciggy remained there until the troop carrier M.V. "Georgic" arrived after a refit. She had previously been used to transport Italian prisoners of war and was sunk in the Bitter Lakes at Suez. In August 1946 Ciggy sailed as a member of the crew of the M.V. "Georgic" and brought the Cheshire Regiment back to Liverpool.

Whilst serving in Singapore, Ciggy played for the Mine Sweeping Flotilla Football Team. This picture was taken in 1946 at Johore Bahru which is situated on the opposite side of the strait from Singapore. Ciggy is in the middle row holding the ball.

After the War there was still a small fishing fleet at Heswall but Parkgate was silted up and those families which wanted to carry on fishing had to moor their nobbies at either Heswall, Thurstaston, or Caldy. Ciggy never went back to fishing. At first he worked at Cammell Lairds shipyard then started a new career in the building industry, eventually going into partnership with his brother Ernie.

Ciggy and Ernie have both lived colourful lives. Ernie, like his father was a very good footballer in his younger days, playing for Heswall F.C. and also Wirral and Cheshire Youth. He was also a talented runner, being Cheshire County Mile Champion for three years running. During the war Ernie sailed in the Atlantic Convoys and also served on landing ships at the invasions of North Africa, Sicily, Italy and Normandy and was also one of the crew who boarded Adolf Hitler's personal yacht, the "Avso Grille". Ernie is still involved in sport as President of Heswall Football Club.

Ciggy has been enjoying a well earned retirement for a few years now. He was, until recent years, the popular and well respected Chairman of the Irby Club before handing over to the present Chairman, Martin Fairclough. Like most men of his generation who have grown up in hard times, lived through war, served in the forces and worked in different industries, he has a great general knowledge. He has worked at jobs and lived through situations most of us only read about. A few pints with Ciggy can be an education as well as an enjoyable couple of hours.

The undermentioned Houses are situate within the Boundaries of the

Civil Parish (Township) of **Upton** | City or Municipal Borough of | Municipal Ward of | Parliamentary Borough of | Town of | Village or Hamlet, &c., of | Local Board, or [Improvement Commissioners District] of | Ecclesiastical

Page 14

1871

No. of Schedule	Road, Street, &c., and No. or Name of House	Houses Inhabited	Houses Uninhabited (U.), or Building (B.)	Name and Surname of each Person	Relation to Head of Family	Condition	Age Males	Age Females	Rank, Profession, or Occupation	Where Born
				Mary Didsbury	Daughter	—		5	Scholar	Cheshire Upton
				James Do	Son	—	3			Do Do
				Robert Do	Do	—	1 mth			Do Do
74	Bushes Hill	1		William Hutton	Head	Mar	33		Ag. Labourer	Do West Kirby
				Catherine Do	Wife	Do		32		Do Do
				Susannah Do	Daughter	—		8	Scholar	Do Do
				James Do	Son	—	6		Do	Do Do
				William Do	Do	—	2			Do Woodchurch
				Sarah Do	Daughter	—		29mo		Do Storeton
75	Do	1		Nancy Gray	Head	Unmar		58	Charwoman	Do Upton
				Margaret Do	foster	Unmar			Do	Do Do
				William Henry William	Do	Do	13		Farmer Servant	Do
				Mary Tracy	Nurse Child	—		5		Lancashire Liverpool
76	Do	1		Joseph Forancen	Head	Mar	32		Painter & Painter	Cheshire Birkenhead
				Mary Do	Wife	Do		30		Lancashire Liverpool
				Mary Collins Do	Daughter	—		9	Scholar	Do
				Joseph Do	Son	—	7		Do	Do
				Charles Do	Do	—	5		Do	Do
				Joseph Do	Do	—	2			Do
				Margaret Do	Daughter	—		10mo		Do
77	Do	1		Peter Evans	Head	Mar	44		Labourer	Cheshire Upton
				Frances Do	Wife	Mar		40	Laundress	Do Greasby
				Mary Do	Daughter	—			Do	Do Watford
				Mary Earl	Widow in law Widow	Widow			Formerly Farmer	Do Pensby

Total of Houses.. **4** | | Total of Males and Females, | **11** | **13** |

* Draw the pen through such of the words as are inappropriate. • Eng-

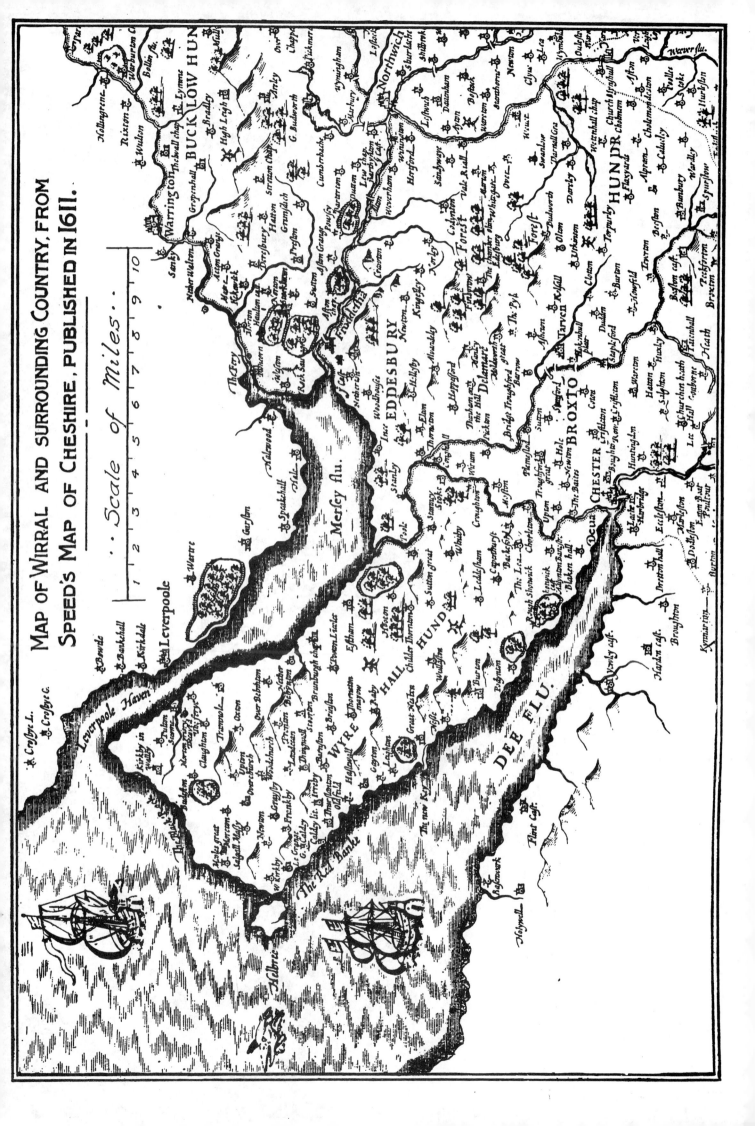

Map of Wirral and Surrounding Country, from Speed's Map of Cheshire, Published in 1611.

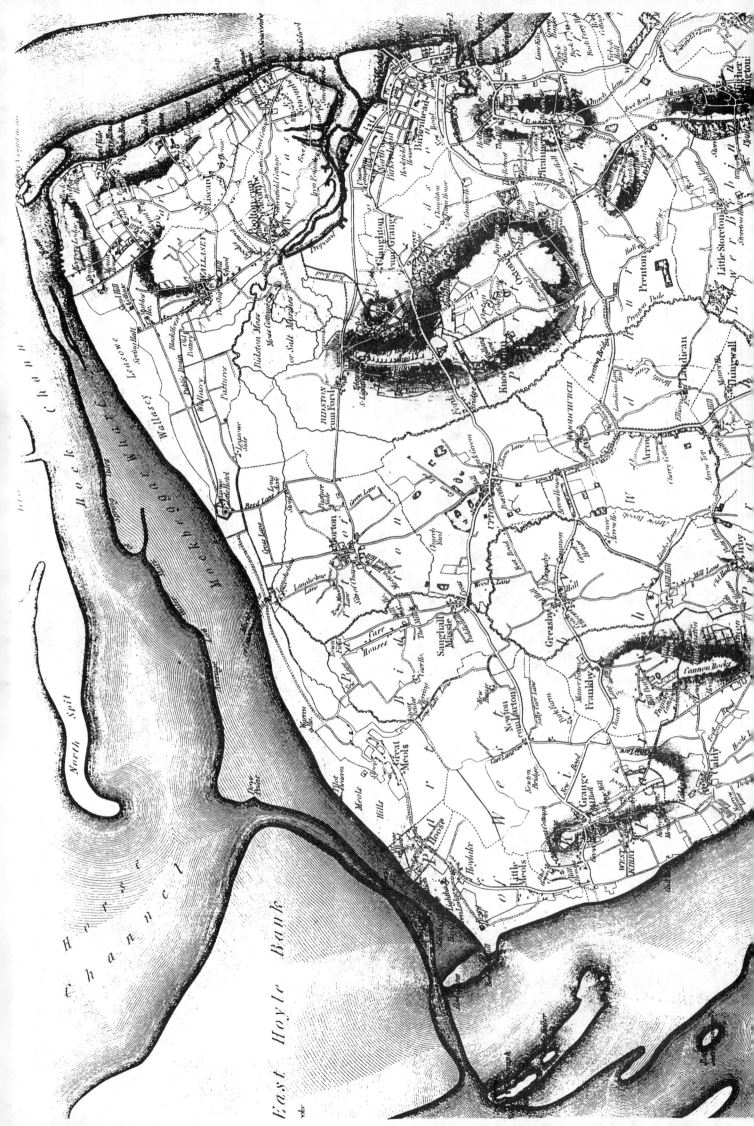

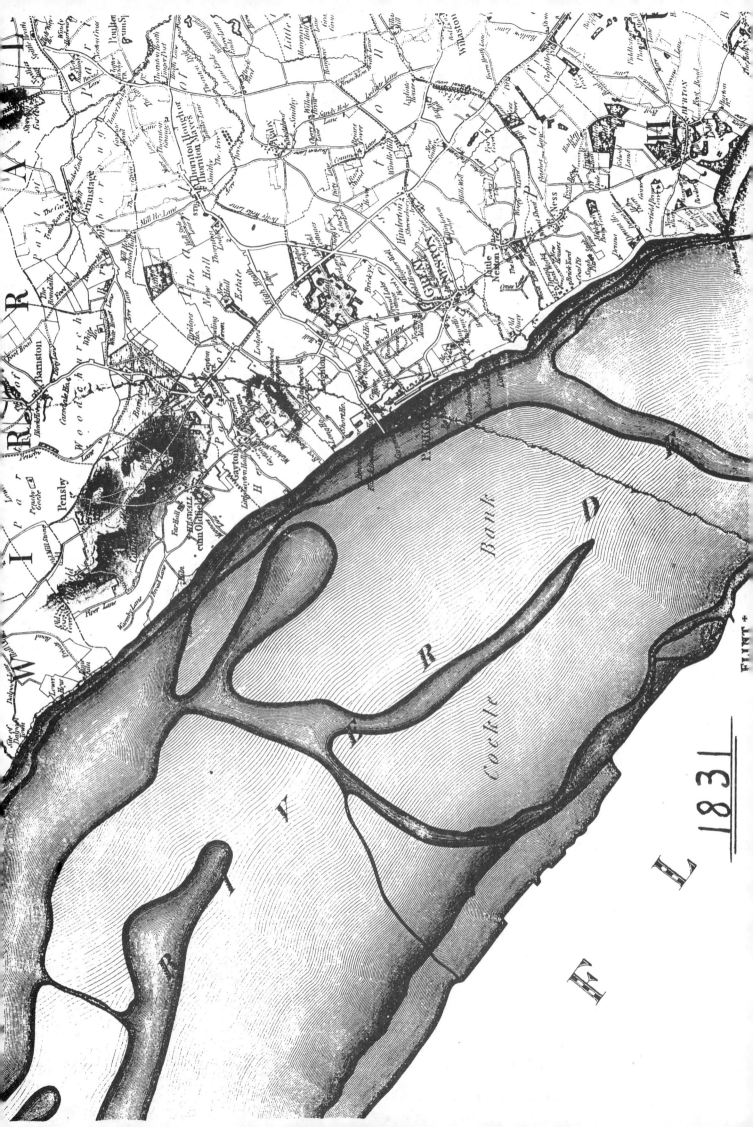

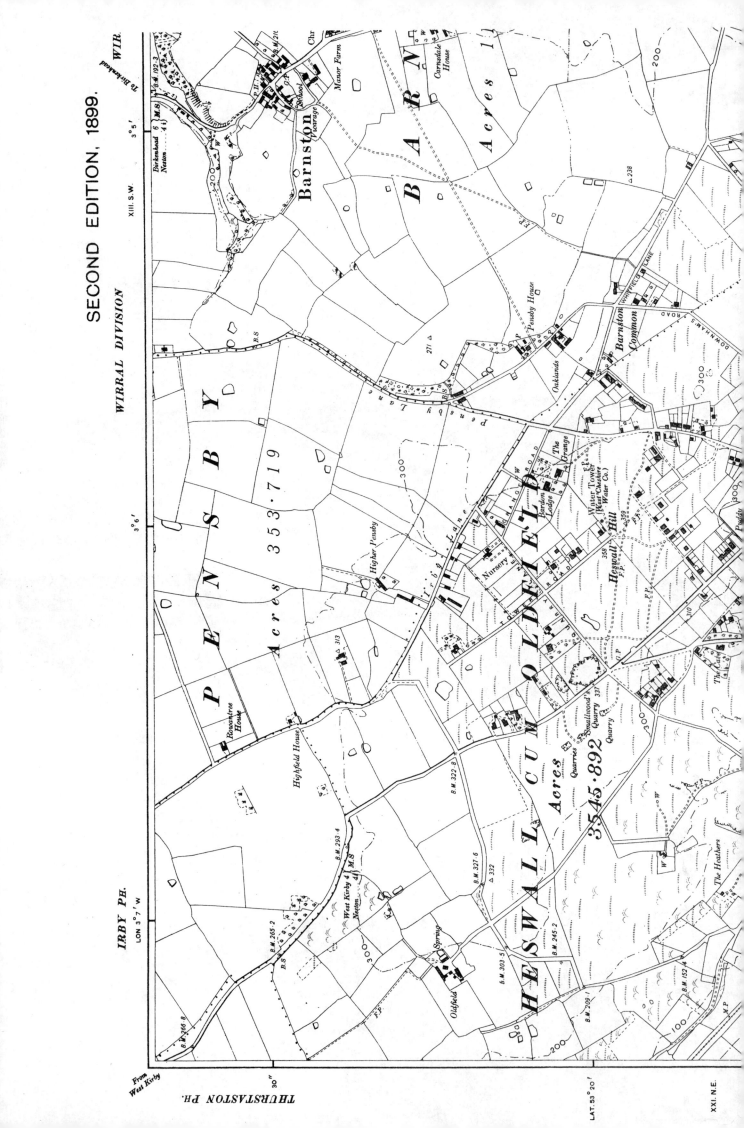

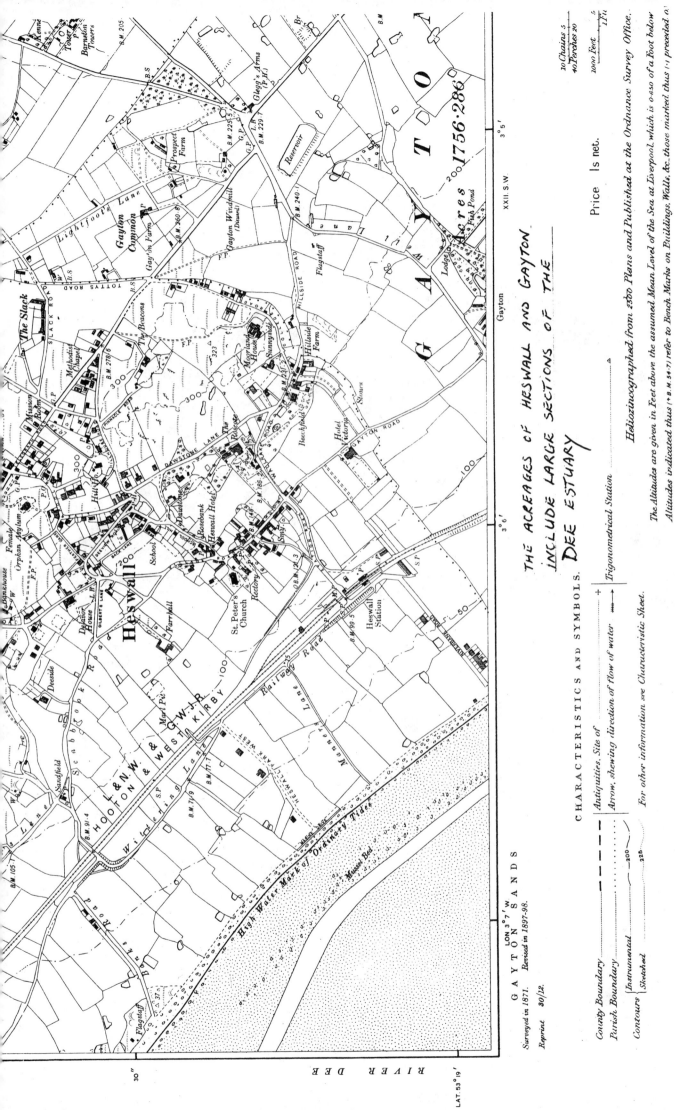

THE ACREAGES OF HESWALL AND GAYTON
INCLUDE LARGE SECTIONS OF THE
DEE ESTUARY

CHARACTERISTICS AND SYMBOLS.

County Boundary — — — —

Parish Boundary ....

Contours { Instrumental ——200——
{ Sketched ——25——

Antiquities, Site of   +

Arrow, shewing direction of flow of water   ⟶

Trigonometrical Station   △

For other information see Characteristic Sheet.

Heliozincographed from 2500 Plans and Published at the Ordnance Survey Office.

The Altitudes are given in Feet above the assumed Mean Level of the Sea at Liverpool, which is 0·430 of a Foot below

Altitudes indicated thus (+B.M. 54·7) refer to Bench Marks on Buildings, Walls, &c.; those marked thus (·) preceded o

Price 1s net.

10 Chains 5
40 Perches 20
1000 Feet
1 Fu

GAYTON SANDS
LON 3° 7' W

Surveyed in 1871. Revised in 1897-98.

Reprint 30/12.

XXII. S.W.

RIVER DEE

LAT. 53° 19'

200 Acres 1756·286

1777

TREE PLANTATIONS AND INCLOSURES 145, 205, 206 AND 207
BECAME THE SITE OF THE CAVE, CAVE COTTAGE, LODGE AND GROUNDS.

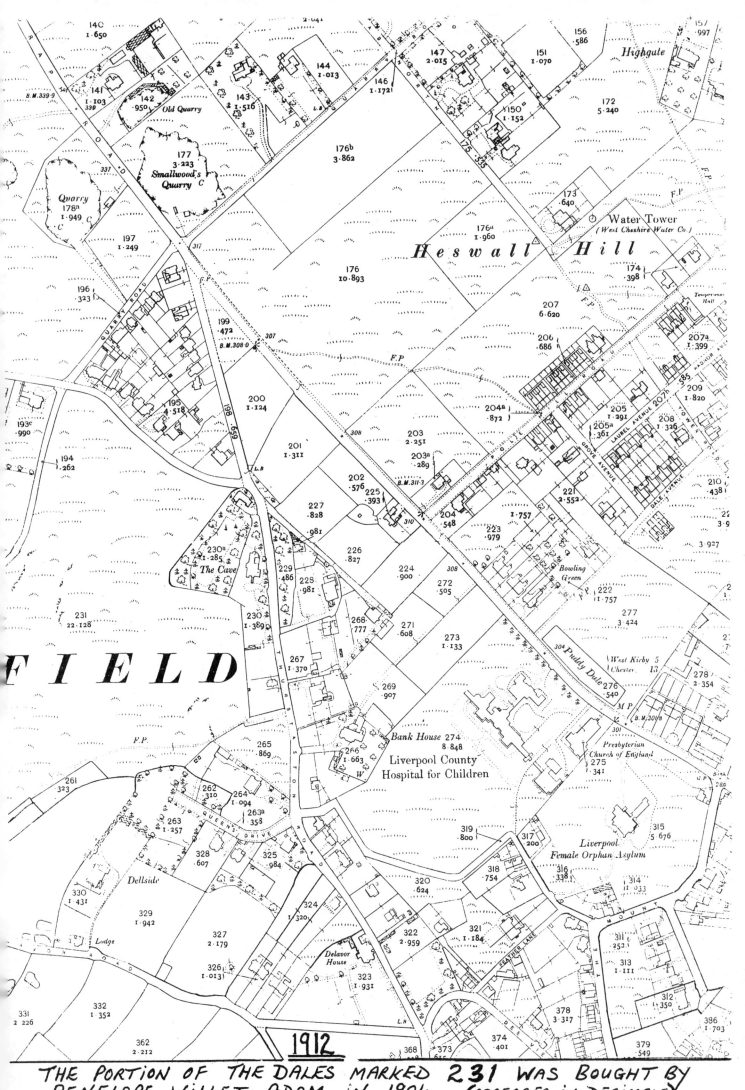

THE PORTION OF THE DALES MARKED **231** WAS BOUGHT BY
PENELOPE WILLET ADAM IN 1904. (ACREAGES IN DECIMALS)

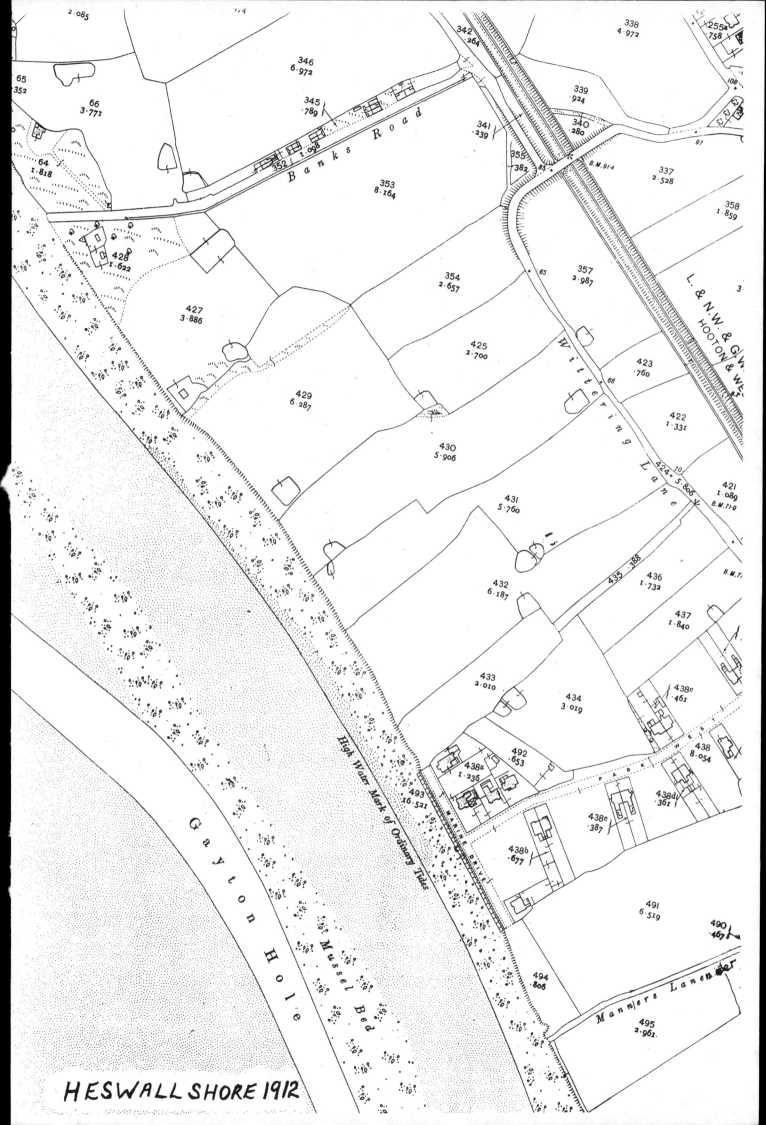

HESWALL SHORE 1912

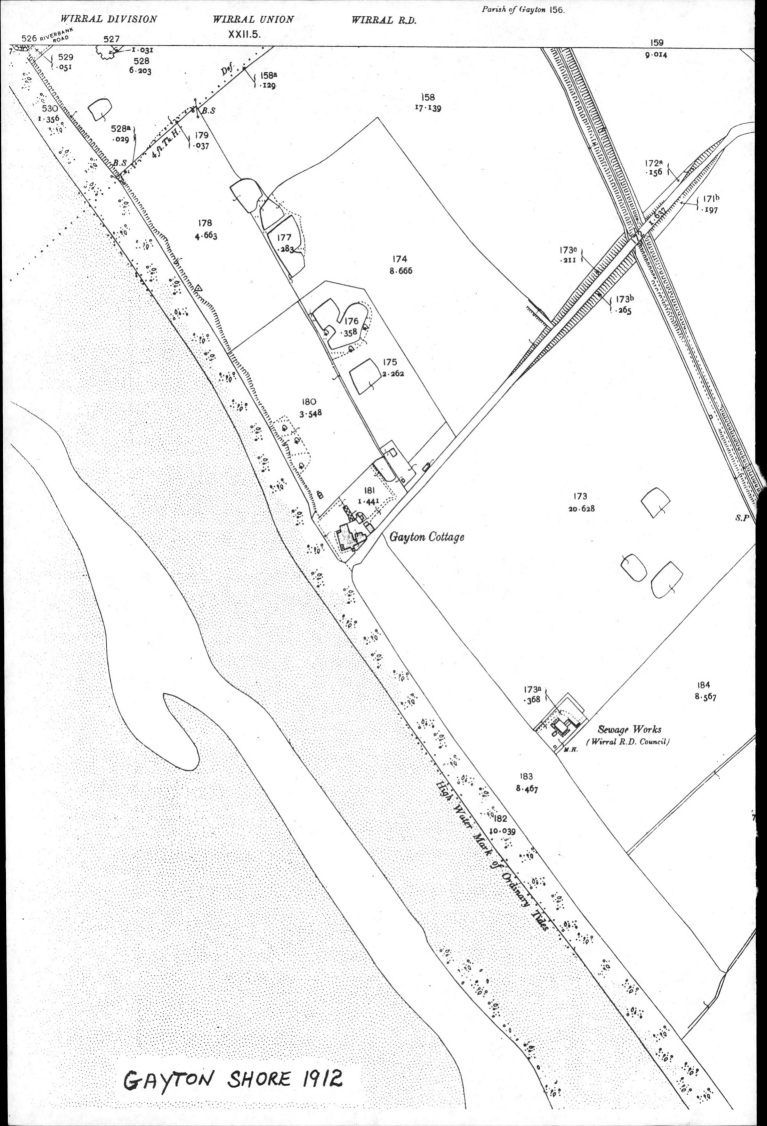

526 RIVERBANK ROAD

527

529
·051

528
6·203

158a
·129

159
9·014

158
17·139

530
1·356

B.S

528a
·029

4 ft. Tk. H.

179
·037

172a
·156

171b
·197

178
4·663

177
·283

174
8·666

173c
·211

·632

173b
·265

176
·358

175
2·262

180
3·548

173
20·628

S.P

181
1·441

Gayton Cottage

173a
·368

184
8·567

Sewage Works
(Wirral R.D. Council)

M.H.

183
8·467

182
10·039

High Water Mark of Ordinary Tides

GAYTON SHORE 1912